Narcissistic and Emotional Abuse

Shattering the Illusion

Anne McCrea

This book is aimed at providing information on narcissistic and emotional abuse.

If you find yourself struggling with issues raised in this book, please do seek professional advice.

Copyright: Anne McCrea 2017

I would like to offer my thanks to Paul Smith who encouraged me to set up the website, NarcissisticandEmotionalAbuse.com, and for his assistance and guidance in doing so. Also, my daughter, Michelle McCrea, who helps me with the website and publishes all the articles and posts and my editor, Paul Feldstein from The Feldstein Agency for keeping me right. I would also like to take this opportunity to thank my son Steven and my life-long friend, Anna Patterson, for listening, and for their continuing support and encouragement, without which, I would never have written this book, which I hope will be informative to all who read it.

INTRODUCTION	8
CHAPTER 1	10

WHAT IS NARCISSISTIC PERSONALITY DISORDER? A Brief Look
COMMON CHARACTERISTICS OF SOMEONE WITH NPD
WHAT IS EMOTIONAL ABUSE?
RED FLAGS OF TOXIC PEOPLE

CHAPTER 2	21

A GLOSSARY OF TERMS RELATED TO NARCISSISM

CHAPTER 3	28

WHO IS A TARGET FOR A NARCISSIST?

CHAPTER 4	30

NARCISSISTIC SUPPLY
NARCISSISTIC ENTITLEMENT

CHAPTER 5	33

THE OVERT NARCISSIST
THE COVERT NARCISSIST

CHAPTER 6	36

IDEALISE, DEVALUE AND DISCARD...
THE PULL AND PUSH IN A RELATIONSHIP WITH A NARCISSIST
THE CYCLE OF MIND CONTROL
DEVALUATION

CHAPTER 7	42

MIRRORING
MANIPULATIVE BEHAVIOUR
GASLIGHTING

CHAPTER 8	48

BAITING

TRIANGULATION
PROJECTION / BLAME SHIFTING

CHAPTER 9   51

NARCISSISTIC INJURY
NARCISSISTIC RAGE
THE SILENT TREATMENT
THE SILENT TREAMENT AND NO CONTACT… WHAT ARE THE DIFFERENCES?

CHAPTER 10   58

ACCOUNTABILITY
THE NARCISSIST AND PATHOLOGICAL LYING

CHAPTER 11   61

THE NARCISSIST'S SMEAR CAMPAIGN
THE BYSTANDER IS AN ENABLER

CHAPTER 12   66

NARCISSISM IN FAMILIES
THE NARCISSISTIC PARENT
HOW DO YOU DEAL WITH THE DEATH OF A NARCISSISTIC PARENT?
THE NARCISSISTIC SIBLING
THE NARCISSISTIC ADULT SON OR DAUGHTER
CO-PARENTING WITH A NARCISSIST
PROTECTING YOUR CHILDREN FROM A NARCISSISTIC PARENT
WHAT CAN YOU DO IF YOUR CHILD BEHAVES IN THIS MANNER?
WHAT HAPPENS IF YOUR KIDS TURN AGAINST YOU?

CHAPTER 13   81

NARCISSISM / MOBBING IN THE WORKPLACE
THE FEMALE NARCISSIST
NARCISSISM AND FRIENDSHIP
THE NARCISSIST IN COURT

CHAPTER 14   88

NARCISSISM AND JEALOUSY

NARCISSISM AND ENVY
NARCISSISTS AND HYPOCRISY
NARCISSISTS AND SELFISHNESS
NARCISSISTS AND THEIR MONEY
NARCISSISTS LOVE TO SPOIL SPECIAL OCCASIONS
NARCISSISTS AND SOCIAL MEDIA

CHAPTER 15 — 96

THE NARCISSIST AND RELIGION
THE NARCISSIST AND APOLOGY
THE NARCISSIST HATES BEING IGNORED
REJECTION AND THE NARCISSIST
LAUGHING AT A NARCISSIST

CHAPTER 16 — 100

THE AGING NARCISSIST
THE NARCISSIST AND ILLNESS
THE NARCISSIST ON THEIR DEATHBED
THE NARCISSIST AND SUICIDE

CHAPTER 17 — 105

HOW A NARCISSIST LOOKS AT LIFE AND YOU

CHAPTER 18 — 107

DO NARCISSISTS REALLY LOVE THEMSELVES?
CAN A NARCISSIST CHANGE?
WHY DO PEOPLE STAY?

CHAPTER 19 — 111

TRAUMA BONDING

CHAPTER 20 — 113

HOOVERING
WHY DID THE NARCISSIST NOT COME BACK TO ME? WHY IS THERE NO HOOVER?

CHAPTER 21 — 116

DO YOU WARN THE NARCISSIST'S NEXT TARGET?
SEEKING REVENGE
EXPOSING A NARCISSIST

CHAPTER 22 — 119

SCAPEGOAT
COGNITIVE DISSONANCE
RUMINATION
CO-DEPENDENCY
EMPATHY.... A RARE GIFT
THE EMPATH AND THE 'WOUNDED' NARCISSIST

CHAPTER 23 — 125

NO CONTACT AND DETACHMENT
BOUNDARIES...YOUR LIFE, YOUR RULES
GREY ROCK

CHAPTER 24 — 130

FORGIVENESS... SHOULD WE FORGIVE?
CLOSURE
BEING ALONE DOESN'T ALWAYS MEAN YOU'RE LONELY

CHAPTER 25 — 135

RECOVERY FROM ABUSE
POST TRAUMATIC STRESS DISORDER
COMPLEX PTSD
COGNITIVE BEHAVIOURAL THERAPY (CBT)
FINDING THE RIGHT THERAPIST

AUTHOR'S NOTE — 141

QUOTES BY ANNE McCREA FROM THE FACEBOOK PAGE AND WEBSITE — 144

REFERENCES — 151

INTRODUCTION

In an ideal world, we would live and interact with kind, considerate folk who have our best interests at heart. Sadly, that is a far cry from the world we live in today. There appears to be an increase in people who are simply out for themselves, people who are controlling and demanding, people who put their needs before those of anyone else, and people who refuse to play by society's rules. They trample on anyone on their way to the top. There are those who need constant attention and admiration, who will put others down to elevate themselves, those who will cause unimaginable pain to those closest to them and show zero empathy, shame or remorse. This world is full of people who will lie, who will destroy someone's reputation, because in their twisted minds, they believe somehow that they deserve it.

Unfortunately, many of these people fly under the radar, hiding their true colours behind a false identity, a false self. To the outside world they appear charismatic and charming, but behind closed doors, they are hostile, manipulative and exploitive. These individuals may appear normal, but they are con artists and master manipulators, who are often believed by those around them. This type of personality frequently displays an air of grandiosity and arrogance, but behind the false exterior there often lies a vulnerability and such a very fragile ego, an ego that is so very easily dented. If you are the one guilty of a 'crime', as they see it, you will pay and pay very dearly. Nothing will ever be their fault. No matter what goes wrong in their lives, they will never self-reflect and admit to the possibility that they may be to blame.

Regrettably, some people who have been abused by this type of personality find themselves not being believed. Abusers will not abuse everyone they encounter. They are selective and have a reputation to uphold. Their reputation is paramount.

People who behave in such a callous manner may have a condition known as Narcissistic Personality Disorder, or NPD. The word 'narcissist' is thrown about rather casually today, but unless you have had the misfortune of dealing with these individuals, you may not know exactly what a narcissist is and the traits they may possess.

I should state here that one needs to be very careful about labelling someone as a narcissist, psychopath or sociopath. These unflattering labels should not be pinned to an individual without just cause and to do so could be slanderous or libellous.

'Narcissists have two faces… their real face, the face they don't want many people to see and the one they put on for display purposes. Those two faces are so totally different. The face you will see depends on how well you know the narcissist. They are skilful actors who can switch on the charm when necessary, fooling those around them into believing that they are kind, considerate and of good character, when the opposite is true. Those closest to them know the truth. Given time, most people eventually see through the dishonesty and the fake persona.'

NPD is difficult to diagnose, even for experts if they do not know the individual personally. Narcissists are known to fool experts into believing that they are, in fact, a victim, rather than the perpetrator.

CHAPTER 1

WHAT IS NARCISSISTIC PERSONALITY DISORDER

A Brief Overview

NPD is a long-term pattern of deviant behaviour considered to be unacceptable by society in general. The narcissist, male or female, often comes across as arrogant, selfish, and conceited with a tendency to look down on other people who they perceive as inferior. They regularly display a sense of entitlement demanding admiration and special treatment. However, below this outward portrayal of confidence and superiority, there are often deep-seated insecurities and self-loathing. Narcissists are renowned for having problematic relationships and a history of alienating family members, friends, associates, work colleagues, customers and just about everyone who they encounter. They are self-centred and egotistical, liking to be the centre of attention, hence, the needs of those around them are of little or no concern. After an encounter with a narcissist, people tend to leave with feelings of anger, betrayal and self-doubt.

'Only a weak and insecure person would feel the need to destroy another human being to make themselves feel better.'

To blend in with society, the narcissist needs to look good from the outside. They need to portray the appearance of being a decent human being. Many people are fooled on first encountering a narcissist, being seduced by their charm, but the longer you know a narcissist, the more apparent their unacceptable behaviour becomes. They will ignore, denigrate and slander others to boost their own position and their insatiable ego. Their complete lack of empathy is profound. They cannot or will not put themselves in someone else's shoes or try to understand someone else's pain or distress. These disordered individuals are motivated by tunnel vision, using and manipulating people for their own ends, to get what they want when they want with no regard for anyone else's feelings or who gets hurt in the process. They will show a pattern of treating people without mercy, one poor soul after another. Narcissists can commit the most despicable and abhorrent acts without feeling the least bit guilty or remorseful.

Their envy speaks for itself. Narcissists will talk behind your back in the hope of turning everyone against you. They don't like to see others being more popular, achieving, making more money or being happier than they are themselves. This envy frequently results in the narcissist spreading lies and malicious gossip in an effort to destroy the innocent person's character, known as a 'Smear Campaign'. I will cover this topic later in the book.

Experts throughout the world use criteria in the Diagnostic and Statistical Manual (DSM) which is published by the American Psychiatric Association, to diagnose mental health conditions such as NPD.

The Mayo Clinic sets out the criteria from the DSM-5 criteria for narcissistic personality disorder:

- Having an exaggerated sense of self-importance.

- Expecting to be recognized as superior even without achievements that warrant it.

- Exaggerating your achievements and talents.

- Being preoccupied with fantasies about success, power, brilliance, beauty or the perfect mate.

- Believing that you are superior and can only be understood by or associate with equally special people.

- Requiring constant admiration.

- Having a sense of entitlement.

- Expecting special favours and unquestioning compliance with your expectations.

- Taking advantage of others to get what you want.

- Having an inability or unwillingness to recognize the needs and feelings of others.

- Being envious of others and believing others envy you.

- Behaving in an arrogant or haughty manner.

Diagnosis is by trained mental health professionals. To be diagnosed with the rather unflattering label of narcissistic personality disorder, one must possess at least five of the traits mentioned. A common and very important trait, which is not mentioned in this list, is that of little or no empathy. There are many who believe that as this is such a key aspect in people with NPD that it should have been included in the diagnostic criteria.

We do not know what causes NPD but there are many theories which include:

- Overvaluing as a child.
- A learned behaviour.
- Genetics.
- Abuse in childhood.

The root cause is more than likely complex with the possibility of a combination of more than one factor being the fundamental reason behind this disorder.

'A narcissist is a great pretender. In the beginning they will pretend to have high morals, compassion, empathy and respect for you. Don't be fooled. They can't keep up this pretence for long as they don't possess any of these qualities. Time will reveal that this was a well-rehearsed deception from the outset.'

COMMON CHARACTERISTICS OF PEOPLE WITH NPD

To someone who has not experienced this type of personality in their lives, the absolute destruction and devastation caused by such personalities is not easily understood. To the target of this insidious abuse, the effects can be devastating, life changing and long lasting.

On first meeting a narcissist, they appear to be likable and charming. They are good at making you feel special, but they are con artists with a secret agenda.

Narcissists are willing to hurt anyone to achieve their goals. During my work in running a Facebook page and website, Narcissistic and Emotional Abuse, I have heard some heart-breaking stories from survivors of narcissistic and emotional abuse. These toxic personalities want power and control. They want everything on their terms, they are control freaks whose motto is, 'My way or the highway'. They manipulate others into behaving as they deem fit, causing chaos where once there was peace and calm. They pit people against each other, twisting words, perhaps with a hint of truth mixed with lies and stirred well. Narcissists often isolate their targets from friends and family. They want them all to themselves without a support network. Then, when the relationship is on shaky ground, their targets will have no one to turn to except them.

There are different types of narcissism and whilst some will display only five of the necessary traits, the more extreme narcissist will tick every box. Equality is not a word in the narcissist's vocabulary. Being regarded as equal to those who they see as subordinate would be demeaning. They are extremely critical of others but are unable to withstand even a little taste of their own medicine.

The narcissist is a pathological liar. They lie compulsively to make their lives appear more interesting, to make others look small, to destroy someone's reputation, to make themselves look better and to play the victim to circumstances they created to gain sympathy. If caught out in their lies, they will tell more, to cover up their lies and deception. They tell the truth in misleading ways to give others incorrect perspectives. A narcissist will contradict themselves on a regular basis, lying about facts and misquoting things that others have said.

Boasting is a common feature in the narcissist's behaviour. They will boast about everything they have done and achieved.

Narcissists lack self-control yet demand the very same from others. Expect an overreaction of uncontrollable rage, similar to a childish temper tantrum, when things don't go their way. Their rage may be fuelled by something as little as a contrary viewpoint. They do not learn from their mistakes and as a result tend to repeat them over and over again.

Someone with NPD is an extremely selfish individual who wants your time and attention when they demand it. They feel that rules don't apply to them. They are risk takers believing that they are above the law and won't get caught.

Narcissists lack morality yet are the first to judge when it comes to the moral standards of others. They often project, criticising you for the very behaviour that they can't or won't accept in themselves. By not facing up to their own inadequacies, they fail to address their weaknesses and failures.
Appealing to their better nature is a waste of time. Waiting for a sincere apology when they have done you wrong is futile.

Some narcissists will overspend and appear to be overly generous to impress others but underneath this false extravagance they are frugal, mean and loathe having to splash out.

Narcissists thrive on drama and love to create chaos, rivalry and division where once there was none.

People who have been around narcissists for any length of time will say that they walk on eggshells for fear of upsetting this fragile personality. They will find that their self-esteem has been slowly and systematically eroded as the narcissist chips away at their confidence and independence.

Any form of criticism cannot be handled by someone who has such a low opinion of themselves. Narcissists have a short fuse with the slightest of criticism being met with punishment such as narcissistic rage or one of their favourite weapons of destruction, a sulking passive aggressive behaviour known as 'The Silent Treatment', where you will be banished from their company and your very presence ignored.

Narcissists will take advantage of kind-hearted people and have an uncanny knack of pushing good people to their very limit. Good people have a breaking point and when the narcissist succeeds, as they so often do, they sit back and watch as you crack under the pressure and torment. You have been deeply hurt, isolated and misunderstood. Your reaction will direct attention away from their monstrous behaviour. Who looks crazy now? Yes, they've got it all worked out. After all they have practised this form of manipulation time and time again.

When other people call them out on their inappropriate, bullying behaviour, they will be considered as jealous or liars and subsequently cast aside.

A narcissist wants you to feel sorry for them. They will paint a picture of how badly they have been treated in the past. Your sympathy gives them the attention they crave and plays on your heart. Your kind nature will dictate that you try so very hard to make sure that they are never hurt like that again. You will do everything in your power to make them feel loved and admired. Be mindful, you will likely be added to that list of evil doers sometime in the future!

The narcissist's acquaintances tend to be rather shallow. They may have people who hang on their every word, aptly named flying monkeys or enablers, whose role is to do the narcissist's bidding. People who spend a lot of time in the narcissist's company usually discover that this person who they once admired is a critical gossip, and get fed up with their behaviour. As time passes, the narcissist is often abandoned when people eventually see their true colours.

Abandonment is one of their biggest fears. The attention that they receive is their very life fuel; without such, they crumble. Like a drug addict without their supply, the narcissist can't cope when supplies become scarce and run out. They become chronically depressed and angry and find no pleasure in anything. Things that they used to enjoy no longer hold their interest. Their world has become hostile, their social life, non-existent. A succession of failed relationships adds to their already fragile ego. They often become a hermit, closed off from the outside world, blaming everyone else for the situation that they find themselves in. They don't like themselves and no one else appears to like them either so why be nice? Everyone who once cared about them is long gone, but the narcissist will blame everyone else but themselves for the situation that they find themselves in.

The question of whether the narcissist personality improves or worsens with age is a very common one. From my research and from the views of those on the Facebook page and website, there is no doubt that for the vast majority, these individuals do indeed worsen with age. Their fragile ego cannot handle what they see in the mirror. The mirror does not lie. Gone are the good looks that they once relied upon (if any existed to begin with). Throughout the years, people have come and gone. They eventually see them for who they really are, the cold and empty shell of a human being beneath the suave exterior. Towards the end of their lives there is often not one single living soul who cares whether they live or die. Call it Karma, call it God having the final say, call it what you will… I call it pay back.

Don't let a narcissist convince you that they care about you. Someone who truly cares about you will never get pleasure from making you feel low. Someone who cares about you will never get power from making you feel weak. Someone who loves you will not want to tear you down and control your life. They will want to see you happy and make you happy, not be the cause of your unhappiness.

Don't fail to see the writing on the wall.

I have written this book to enlighten people on the topic of narcissistic behaviour and emotional abuse, the signs to look out for, and the various terms and behaviour that you may encounter. The terms narcissist and emotional abuse are thrown about a lot these days. Not everyone who is abusive at times will be considered a narcissist. They may simply be toxic and best avoided.

Learning about the behaviour of a narcissist and why they do what they do is a very important aspect of the recovery process. Many people leave relationships involving a narcissistic personality feeling absolutely devastated and confused with no understanding of what has just happened. They have no idea that they were dealing with a narcissistic individual. Many are dealing with feelings of self-blame and deep hurt. They have been conditioned by the narcissist to accept responsibility when things go wrong, so when the relationship is over, they often shoulder the blame, wondering what it was that they did wrong. They have no notion that this is the way these relationships are destined to end from the very beginning. Relationships with narcissists tend to follow a pattern known as *idealize, devalue and discard.* I will discuss this topic later in the book.

Hopefully, after reading this book, you will gain insight into the mind of a narcissist, become aware of red flags to look out for in toxic personalities and subsequently recognize their behaviour and take appropriate steps to protect yourself.

WHAT IS EMOTIONAL ABUSE?

Emotional abuse may be referred to as psychological violence or mental abuse, which involves subjecting someone to behaviour which may result in psychological distress or trauma such as chronic depression, stress, anxiety and post-traumatic stress disorder. Emotional abuse can be just as devastating as physical abuse, sometimes even more so. How do you know if you are being emotionally abused? The answer is in the way a person makes you feel as a result of their behaviour. If someone controls your life, puts you down and creates feelings of low self-worth, you are being abused. If someone is stopping you from being yourself, expressing yourself or isolating you from your friends and family, you are being emotionally abused.

Examples of emotional abuse include:

- Aggressive behaviour towards you.
- Controlling behaviour.
- Criticism.
- Making you feel bad about yourself.
- Isolating you from friends and family.
- Name calling.
- Being made to feel guilty.
- Giving you the silent treatment.
- Financial abuse.

The aim of an emotional abuser is to gradually chip away at your self-esteem and independence so that, in time, you become a shell of your former self. Eventually, you may feel trapped with no way out of the relationship. You may feel that you can't manage without this abusive person in your life. You can, and you will. These feelings are due to a psychological phenomenon known as *trauma bonding* which I will cover later in the book.

RED FLAGS OF TOXIC PEOPLE

Not all toxic people are narcissists, but we still need to keep these people at arm's length and not be drawn into their toxicity.

There are often red flags that we should never ignore which can tell us a lot about a person. How many times do we see something at the start of a relationship and ignore it thinking it was a 'one off'? By the time we see the next one, we've almost forgotten about the first! Please keep them logged in your head. One or two instances may not indicate that someone is truly toxic but when these little red flags are waved in front of you time and time again, they become a massive warning sign of a treacherous path ahead.

1. This person makes you feel on edge. You can't really put your finger on the reason but you've no doubt there's something not quite right.

2. They are rude or talk down to a waiter.

3. They get too close far too soon. Love doesn't normally work that way. It takes time for bonds to form and love to grow.

4. They are charming to the point of being beyond the realms of normality. Trust that old saying, 'If something appears too good to be true, it probably is'.

5. They tell you of how their previous partners cheated, lied, were crazy etc. They play the victim and have got you feeling sorry for them. It wasn't their fault. Yes, you've got it... They are the common denominator. They are likely to be the one with the problem.

6. They have a short supply of genuine friends. Friends don't usually hang around toxic people for lengthy periods of time.

7. You do most of the talking. They do the listening, figuring you out, knowing your likes and dislikes so they can pretend to be the person you want them to be. However, once the relationship is established, they switch to talking about themselves which of course is a much more interesting subject!

8. They criticise your friends and family hoping to create the division that will eventually lead to your isolation from everyone you once held dear.

9. Although critical of others, they can't stand a taste of their own medicine, being extremely sensitive to any form of criticism.

10. You find yourself being compared to ex friends, ex partners and family.

11. They rarely have anything good to say about anyone.

12. You feel you have to walk on eggshells around this person.

13. They demand most of your time.

14. They hate to be alone. They need people to provide them with their much-needed narcissistic supply. Being alone allows too much time for self-reflection.

15. They don't respect your boundaries.

16. They use passive aggressive behaviour, such as the cold shoulder, stonewalling and the silent treatment, in response to perceived slight.

17. They have an uncontrollable rage/anger.

18. They are pathological liars. They lie even when there's absolutely no need to and the truth would be a better option.

19. Nothing is ever their fault. They never accept responsibility for their faults or accept blame for anything untoward.

20. They cause chaos where there was once peace and calm. (Divide and conquer).

21. They lack morals yet expects yours to be high.

22. They insult you and if you are offended, they tell you that you're being much too sensitive.

23. They suggest what you should wear, how you should do your hair... Once again, this is all about control.

24. They show their true colours to you whilst maintaining their 'charm' to the outside world.

25. They lack empathy and are either unable or unwilling to put themselves in someone else's shoes.

26. They are constantly seeking compliments

27. They have a grandiose view of themselves. However, underneath their grandiosity, may lie a low self-esteem.

28. They think that they have the ability to know what you are thinking.

29. They are envious of others' possessions and/or accomplishments.

30. They like to be the centre of attention, expecting your praise for minor achievements; expecting their needs to be met, after all, theirs are much more important than yours.

31. They are a serial flirter.

32. They show no remorse.

33. If they treat you badly, you must have done something to deserve it!

34. They have a strong sense of entitlement.

35. They are jealous of close relationships that you may have.

36. They possess the most fragile of egos.

37. They act like they are above the law; rules don't apply to them.

38. They rarely apologise, and if they do, it's either insincere or in their best interests to do so.

39. They believe they can only be understood by high achieving important people, like themselves.

40. They are in good form one minute and in bad form the next.

41. They hold grudges/hatred for a lifetime against those who they believe have wronged them in some way.

42. They are preoccupied with their image, always wanting to look good in front of others.

43. They don't express genuine emotions.

To preserve your health and your sanity, keep your distance from toxic people as far as humanly possible. There are generally two sides to every story. There is the truth and then there is the toxic person's version. Their version rarely comes close when it comes to the truth and their flying monkeys, or enablers, pass judgement without listening to both sides of the story. Be patient. No one can hide from the truth for ever.

CHAPTER 2

A GLOSSARY OF TERMS RELATED TO NARCISSISM

ACON

Adult Children of Narcissists

BAITING

A narcissist loves to provoke a reaction from you, especially in public. They will provoke you into responding in an angry or emotional manner. (Your angry response is further evidence of your unbalanced state of mind).

BLACK SHEEP

The black sheep is blamed for just about everything that goes wrong within the dysfunctional family. They can't do anything right. Their achievements are not recognized by the narcissistic parent and are swept under the carpet.

BOUNDARIES

Boundaries are a code of conduct or an unwritten set of rules which we consider to be reasonable behaviour from those around us and our response when someone steps over the line.

CLOSURE

Closure in a normal relationship involves open and honest communication about what has gone wrong, you then wish each other well, say goodbye and move on. After a relationship with a narcissist ends you are left with so many questions and no answers. It feels like the book has been closed before the story has ended. We cannot expect any form of closure from the emotionally immature narcissist who is completely lacking in empathy, and has no regard for your feelings. The only closure in this type of relationship is the closure you give yourself.

CO-DEPENDENT

The individual characteristics vary from person to person. Some of the more common characteristics would include trying to avoid making decisions, preferring to rely on others. Co-dependents are often perfectionists who tend to put the needs of others above their own, which results in them feeling needed.

Unfortunately, co-dependents often stay in relationships that are emotionally destructive or abusive.

COUNTERING

A narcissist will dismiss or nullify their target's thoughts, feelings or experiences and make them feel that they are wrong to hold such feelings or thoughts.

COGNITIVE DISSONANCE

Cognitive dissonance occurs when one holds two or more contradictory beliefs or values at the same time.

Sometimes people hold very strong beliefs and when they are presented with evidence which opposes those beliefs, they find it impossible to accept this evidence. Dissonance is often strong when we go against our own moral standards, for example, if someone believes that they are a good person and goes ahead and does something wrong or bad, the feelings of guilt and discomfort are known as cognitive dissonance.

DUPLICITY

Deception by speaking or acting in two different ways to different people about the same subject. Dishonest behaviour.

DISSOCIATION

Dissociation from mild to moderate is a detachment from reality, usually in the case of abuse. It is a defence mechanism.

DISCOUNTING

A target of abuse is denied the right to hold their own feelings. For example, being told that you are much too sensitive or have no sense of humour, thereby invalidating your reality.

EMOTIONAL ABUSE

Emotional abuse may be referred to as psychological violence or mental abuse, which involves subjecting someone to behaviour which may result in psychological distress or trauma such as chronic depression, stress, anxiety and post-traumatic stress disorder.

ENABLER

An enabler is someone who, by their action or inaction, encourages or enables a pattern of behaviour to continue, or removes the consequences of bad behaviour.

FALSE GUILT

False guilt is guilt that someone places on themselves because of their perceived failures or inadequacies. If they have not broken a 'moral law' and feel guilty, this is known as false guilt.

FALSE FLATTERY

Narcissists love to be admired and receive compliments, so they assume that everyone needs this too. They will tell you that you are special, no one can understand them like you do and put you on a pedestal. I'm not saying that you are not special but don't be fooled by their compliments. They are all part of the game!

FALSE SELF

The narcissist creates a false image of his or herself. This image is not a reflection of their true character. They will display this image to impress and mislead others, knowing that their real self, the person who they really are, is not likely to impress anyone. This false image is not likely to be maintained for a lengthy period of time.

FALSE VULNERABILITY

The narcissist often pretends that they need you. This makes you feel good about yourself, an important part of their lives. You are important to them for as long as you give them the attention they need, but replaceable when you don't.

FLYING MONKEYS

Flying monkeys are people who have been convinced by the narcissist that he or she is the real victim. They inflict further harm on the real victim by submitting to the narcissist's wishes and demands. They may threaten, torment, discredit or add fuel to a smear campaign by spreading lies and gossip.

GAS-LIGHTING

Gas-lighting is a manipulative tactic where a mentally healthy individual is subjected to conditioning behaviour so that they doubt their own sanity. The target starts to believe that their perception of reality is false. The narcissist may simply deny saying something didn't happen when in fact, it did, telling you that you heard wrong or lie about an event or situation. Over time a victim starts to think they are confused and going crazy. They come to rely more and more on the narcissist to keep them right.

GOLDEN CHILD

The golden child can do no wrong, will be encouraged to do well and be given the best of everything. The narcissistic parent will celebrate even their most minor achievements whilst their faults and failings are swept under the carpet. This child may receive special treatment for being the perfect child and for doing everything that their parent wishes.

GRANDIOSITY

An unrealistic sense of superiority. A grandiose narcissist sees themselves as better than others and views other people with disdain.

GREY ROCK

Grey rock is a term used to describe your behaviour when trying to cut contact with a narcissist. The aim is to be utterly boring so that the narcissist no longer sees you as good supply and subsequently disappears. Grey Rock differs from no contact in that you don't avoid the narcissist. Instead you keep contact, albeit to a minimum, but keep your responses so extremely boring that the narcissist will see you as a poor source of supply. Your aim is to blend into the background, become insignificant and be as boring as you can possibly be. Talk about the most boring topics you can imagine such as ironing, doing the laundry or how you enjoy watching paint dry. No-one wants to be in the company of boring people and the narcissist is no different.

HOOVERING

The term hoovering, derived from the Hoover vacuum cleaner, describes how a narcissist attempts to suck their victims back into a relationship. They will use every trick in the book to get you back under their power and control. Hoovering often takes place after you have left them or after a period of the silent treatment.

They promise to change their behaviour or say that they have already changed dramatically.

INVALIDATION

Invalidation is a manipulative tactic used to get a target to believe that their thoughts, opinions and beliefs are wrong, unimportant or don't matter.

LOVE BOMBING

Love bombing is a term used to describe the typical initial stages of a relationship with a narcissistic personality, in which the narcissist goes all out to impress their target with flattery, holidays, promises of a future together, having the target believe that they have met their perfect partner, their soulmate.

MIRRORING

A narcissist will mirror what they see in you from your mannerisms to your dress sense, your behaviour and your likes and dislikes. They basically become just like you.

NARCISSISTIC INJURY

A narcissistic injury can be described as any perceived slight, threat or criticism, whether real or in the narcissist's imagination, which they view as an insult, an act of rejection or disagreement.

NARCISSISTIC RAGE

Narcissistic rage is a narcissist's reaction to a narcissistic injury, usually a rather aggressive response which may be likened to a child's temper tantrum. This outward display of rage is normally directed towards whoever the narcissist feels has been the cause of their hurt. On occasion, the rage can be directed towards themselves, where they take the criticism and turn it inward, so they feel a sense of shame and depression.

NARCISSISTIC SUPPLY

A narcissist is lost without narcissistic supply. They need supply like a plant needs water. Supply consists of attention, admiration, respect, adulation and even fear. However, it should be noted that a narcissist can draw on negative supply such as detestation and hatred. Without these vital nutrients of life, the narcissist will become dysfunctional.

NO CONTACT

No contact is put in place by a victim to give themselves time to recover. It is not, in any way, like the narcissist's silent treatment. A narcissist who initiates the silent treatment is doing so as a punishment and to exert power and control.

No contact is a self-imposed set of rules whereby there will be absolutely no contact with the toxic person. (No texts, no emails, no phone calls, no snooping on social media). It has been likened to building a wall between you and a toxic individual. You will not care or even be aware of what happens on the other side of this wall.

(Minimal contact is advised in circumstances where one has to co-parent with a narcissist).

PROJECTION

A narcissist is an expert at projecting their own character flaws or bad behaviour onto others.

They will go to any lengths to avoid being held accountable for any wrong doing and will blame others for the very things that they do themselves. The main objective is to make themselves feel superior, displace responsibility and place it on the shoulders of their unsuspecting target.

PROTECTION GUARANTEE

They may promise to keep you safe from the world. This may make you feel dependent on them for your own safety.

RUMINATION

Rumination can be described as a chain of repetitive thoughts which focus your attention on the symptoms of your distress, personal loss, depression and/or anxiety. Instead of focusing on solutions, your focus is drawn to the possible causes and consequences. Healthy alternatives to rumination are positive distractions, things that take your mind off your problems.

SCAPEGOAT

The scapegoat is someone (or group of people) who is unfairly blamed for the wrongdoings, failures, mistakes and faults of others. A child in a family may be singled out and subjected to unwarranted negative treatment.

SELF ESTEEM

Self-esteem is the overall judgement one holds about their own self-worth, including pride in oneself, self-respect and self-assurance.

STRINGS ATTACHED

There's a reason for everything a narcissist does. If they do something for you, they will remind you somewhere down the line. They will want something from you in return.

TRAUMA BONDING

This term comes from a real-life hostage situation where several of the hostages became emotionally attached to their kidnappers (The Stockholm Syndrome). Trauma bonding is a misplaced loyalty where a victim is emotionally bonded with their abuser and finds themselves unable to leave an unhealthy or dangerous relationship. The victim remains loyal to someone who has betrayed them time and time again.

TRIANGULATION

Narcissists thrive on chaos. They provoke rivalry and jealousy between people, creating triangles to boost their own ego.

VUNERABLE NARCISSIST

The vulnerable narcissist has a very low self-esteem and is constantly on the lookout for proof of their worthiness. This type of narcissist hides behind a mask which masks their deep- seated feelings of insecurity and self-doubt. They are haunted by fears of rejection and abandonment.

CHAPTER 3

WHO IS A TARGET FOR A NARCISSIST?

Anyone can be a target of a narcissistic personality.

The greatest source of narcissistic supply will come from conquering the unconquerable! If they can manipulate someone who can advance their status, this would be considered a great achievement.

I look at this from the mind-set of a mountaineer. At the beginning of their quests to climb mountains, the mountaineer will start off small, and with every successful climb, they will want to go higher the next time. Eventually, they won't get satisfaction unless their climb is more difficult and more challenging than the one before. Their life goal will be to conquer the biggest and the highest mountain. The narcissist's greatest challenge and achievement will be to conquer the strong and powerful. Once having achieved their goal, the narcissist will attempt to tear down those very same attributes that attracted them in the first place.

Under the mask of the narcissist, is often a person of rather low self-esteem, even though to many, they may appear to be confident and assertive. They need to have their fragile egos fed, having a regular source of narcissistic supply which in turn makes them feel superior. They want others to be envious of them and their chosen partner. Narcissists generally do not have any respect for weakness of character. However, weak people who are easily manipulated are seen as soft targets, and the narcissist may choose someone who is sad or insecure on a temporary basis, until someone better comes along, when they will unceremoniously cast aside and dump the weak person.

The narcissist will feel threatened by those who are more popular than themselves and those who they believe to have integrity and strong morals. In some cases, the narcissist will target such people, for no other purpose than to bring them down.

Once the narcissist has picked their target, they will go all out to prove to this person that they have met their soulmate. Their goal will be to make this totally independent, strong person, utterly dependant on them. They will have to work hard to rise to the challenge but once accomplished, imagine the boost to their ego. Once they have you where they want you, they will slowly but surely chip away at your self-confidence so that eventually you become a shadow of your former self.

The narcissist is attracted to the self-sufficient, independent individuals as they will be less likely to have to take care of their needs.

Narcissists are envious of those who are happy and content. If you have a passion for life, they will try to make sure that it won't last long. How dare you be happy, when they find it impossible to ever find such a state of contentment? They will seek to destroy your happiness just to make themselves feel better.

Narcissists don't like being upstaged in any way. If you are the type of person who doesn't feel the need to take centre stage, you'll fit the bill for a time. You will be less likely to take the spotlight away from them.

If you are a perfectionist, you may be targeted because you will want everything to be perfect and you will go out of your way to achieve perfection. You will want to receive their approval for a job well done, but as an acknowledgment is extremely unlikely, you'll try harder next time. You always try to please, doubting yourself and thinking that whatever you do is never good enough.

As discussed in the previous chapter, the narcissist will pray on the empathetic people in this world, the most compassionate, loving and kind people. Someone with such a kind and forgiving nature is much more likely to forgive them time and time again.

Sometimes, if strong, independent targets are unavailable as a source of supply, the narcissist will choose someone who will be an easy target for their manipulation, someone who they see as weak, someone who may be recently divorced or someone in mourning. The depths of their immorality and depravity knows no bounds. Exploiting the vulnerable will give them a lesser degree of supply, but it will be enough until a new source of supply has been established.

CHAPTER 4

NARCISSISTIC SUPPLY

When reading about narcissism, the term *narcissistic supply* is one which you will come across often. A narcissist is addicted to narcissistic supply like a drug addict is addicted to their drug of choice. This supply is attention, adoration, admiration, respect and love etc. However, it should be noted that a narcissist can draw on negative supply such as detestation and hatred. This pathological need for attention, whether good or bad, is vital for their survival, but they do not consider the feelings or opinions of others in their never-ending quest to obtain such supply.

Although the narcissist gives the impression of being strong and independent, they need contact with others, more than any normal individual, to survive, people who will provide a constant stream of attention, admiration and adoration. This supply brings adulation making them feel good about themselves. People are there to supply the narcissist with their 'life blood'.

The following are examples of positive narcissistic supply:

- Admiration.
- Attention.
- Love.
- Respect.
- Devotion.
- Being worshiped.
- Being praised.
- Compliments.
- Being feared.
- Being honoured.

- Wealth.
- Sexual conquests.
- Being recognized for achievements.

Negative supply includes:

- Detestation.
- Hatred.
- Animosity.
- Loathing.

Healthy, normal people enjoy the odd compliment but don't need to be constantly praised and admired. In fact, someone being over the top with compliments would be rather off-putting. Narcissists, on the other hand, thrive on the compliments and can't get enough of them. Due to some narcissistic individuals having a low opinion of themselves, they rely on this adulation and admiration to boost their self-esteem.

The narcissist displays a false self to obtain their narcissistic supply. The false self is an act put on to fool the outside world. Those closest to them know that the true personality of this individual is nothing like the false image portrayed. However, it is this false image which gains the narcissist their much need admiration, adoration, fear and respect, in other words, their narcissistic supply.

NARCISSISTIC ENTITLEMENT

'A narcissist has a strong sense of entitlement, believing that they deserve special treatment. Their demands will be high, yet their investment will be low. It doesn't matter how much you do for them…Nothing will ever be enough.'

As normal people progress from childhood and adolescence into adulthood, most leave behind the childish temper tantrums, the stomping feet, yelling and crying to get what they want, and develop a more mature and refined manner. They gain patience and understanding and, with maturity, learn that not everything will go their way all the time. Sadly, people with narcissistic personality disorder cannot be considered 'normal' by any stretch of the imagination and never seem to move beyond their childish ways, believing that the world evolves around them.

A sense of entitlement is:

- Having an unrealistic belief that one has a right to have, do, or get something.

- The expectation or belief that you deserve special treatment/privileges).

Someone with narcissistic personality disorder has an extremely overblown sense of entitlement. They are ruthless in their quest to ensure that their needs, which are more important than those of anyone else, are met. Woe betide anyone who stands in the way of the narcissist and their goal. They don't have any sense of shame when it comes to trampling over others to achieve their desires.

During conversations in public, the narcissistic personality feels entitled to interrupt when other people are talking. After all, it's difficult to be the centre of attention when other people have taken centre stage.

In their minds they need to get what they want, when and how they want.

What happens when they sate their appetite? It won't be enough... they'll crave more. The narcissist is never satisfied because the goal posts are always moved.

The word, 'compromise' is not a word in the narcissist's vocabulary. Someone with such an acute sense of entitlement doesn't want to meet anyone half way and will push the boundaries until they get their own way. Rules don't apply to them. It's their way or the highway.

To normal people this kind of behaviour comes across as incredibly selfish, and it is. The needs of those around the narcissistic personality are of little or no consequence and are pushed to the bottom of the queue. Sometimes a narcissist can come across as a generous, kind and gentle soul, usually at the outset of a relationship. Don't be fooled. Their apparent kindness and generosity are a ruse, created when there is something in it for them. They give in order to get.

'A normal healthy person will never feel the need to control you. They won't isolate you from your friends and family. They would never dream of humiliating you in public or make you feel guilty when they've done you wrong and they will never get pleasure from being the cause of your pain. Respect yourself enough to let people go.'

CHAPTER 5

THE OVERT NARCISSIST

The overt narcissist is the most obvious of narcissistic personality disorders. He or she is boastful, arrogant and demanding in the extreme. They need admiration and demand special treatment. They have a pathological need for power and control and will be ruthless in their quest to obtain both.

They have unrealistic notions of what they see as their outstanding success in all aspects of their lives. These grandiose narcissists are so full of self-importance, believing that they can only be understood by people of similar high standing. Should their accomplishments fall short they will exaggerate their achievements to obtain the respect and admiration they believe they are entitled to.

When they are not being treated with the deference that they believe they deserve, the overt narcissist is likely to react with rage. Other people are seen to exist only to meet their needs and desires. They don't give a second thought to the needs of those around them.

The overt narcissist is easily offended and doesn't respond well to even the slightest of criticism. Although they generally will not display their rage in public, some will do so if unable to control their anger. Their rage bubbles beneath the surface, ready to explode if criticised or if they don't get their own way. Public displays of their narcissistic rage may lead them to feelings of shame, suicidal thoughts and acts of revenge on the person who they believe is to blame for their outburst. Don't be fooled, there will always be someone to blame for their behaviour.

The overt narcissist is strongly lacking in empathy. Their own feeling of worthlessness leads them to be disturbingly envious of others. If they see someone being more popular, more admired than themselves, they will mimic those qualities that they are envious of, claiming them as their own. They see themselves as superior and will exploit any weaknesses they see in others. By treating others with such contempt, it is not surprising that they have difficulty in maintaining long lasting relationships.

'No matter how hard I tried, I could never understand how anyone could be so intentionally cold and cruel…
And then I knew, I knew that if I had understood their darkness, I would have been just like them.

*I learned that it's not for me to figure them out
And their dysfunction is not my burden to carry.'*

THE COVERT NARCISSIST

Who would believe that the man who sits in church with his perfect family every Sunday is a monster behind closed doors?

No one would believe that the 'doting' mother cheering on her child in the school gala had been yelling and belittling her daughter minutes beforehand.

Who would believe that the friendly local grocer who chats happily with his customers has been giving his wife the silent treatment and not acknowledged her existence for weeks?

Who would believe that the lovely charming 'lady' at the top of her profession trampled on anyone who stood in her way on her rise to the top?

The covert narcissist is a great pretender, hiding who they really are with expertise. The covert narcissist puts on such a convincing display of being a loving, kind person in public but to those who know them personally, to those closest to them, they are selfish, manipulative, exploitive and anything but the loving and kind person that they purport to be. They know that if they displayed their true colours in public, they would lose the recognition, respect and admiration that they so desperately crave. Their ability to fool the outside world makes this type of personality one of the most dangerous, often manifesting in them leading different lives at the same time. They worry about being found out. They are deeply envious of others, knowing that they can never be the person that others believe them to be.

The covert narcissist is a secretive con artist, a master of what he or she does, who lacks the confidence of the overt narcissist. They need constant attention, moving from one relationship to another to avoid being alone. Time spent alone often leads to depression when their needs are not being met. Narcissistic supply is vital to their well-being.

Your value in the narcissist's life will depend on your usefulness. When you are no longer regarded as useful or you challenge them about who they really are, you will be cast aside without a second thought, as if you never existed. Your reputation will have been discredited so that you will never be believed.

The traits of the overt narcissist can be obvious, often being displayed quite openly, but in contrast, the traits of the covert narcissist can be very difficult to spot. Below are some signs that you may be dealing with a covert narcissist...

- Always plays the victim, wanting your sympathy.

- Quiet smugness/superiority.

- Self-absorbed.

- Extreme selfishness.

- Constant craving for acknowledgement.

- Passive aggressive.

- Judgemental and critical.

- Lacks empathy.

- Highly sensitive, unable to handle criticism.

- Difficulties with relationships.

- Gets bored easily.

- Switches off rather than listen intently to others.

Never blame yourself for being deceived by a covert narcissist. They have been known to fool medical professionals. When their marriages have fallen apart they can fool the therapists into believing that they are doing everything in their power to repair their marriage while shifting the blame onto their spouse.

It can be difficult not to get sucked in to a narcissist's web of deceit and feel sorry for them when they play the victim card. The narcissist is looking for a reaction from you. Don't feed the monster! When they fail to get their desired reaction from you, they will take a step back and look for their supply elsewhere. Be aware of the traits before it's too late and don't let yourself be controlled by someone whose ultimate goals are to tear you down and control not only your mind but your life.

CHAPTER 6

IDEALIZE, DEVALUE AND DISCARD

Most people who enter into a romantic relationship do so in the hope of finding lasting love with another human being. They have a mutual respect, empathy, emotional attachment and all the other feelings that go hand in hand with a healthy, normal relationship. A relationship with a narcissist is anything but normal. Their emotional maturity has not developed in the normal way and as a result they become emotionally stunted adults unable to sustain a long lasting, mutually loving and respectful bond with another person.

A typical relationship with someone who has NPD will follow three phases:

- Idealise
- Devalue
- Discard

Phase 1

Idealise or Love Bombing Stage

Idealization is a psychological or mental process of attributing overly positive qualities to oneself or others. It is a seductive process where a manipulative person will set out to control another by a '*toxic whirlwind*' (influencing someone with displays of affection, attention, adoration, gifts and promises of a bright future).

When you first meet a narcissist, whether they are male or female, they will lavish you with attention and bowl you over with their charm and charisma. They have played this part before and they'll dazzle you with their marvellous performance.

You become quickly infatuated and led into the false belief that you have met your soulmate. They give you the impression that they are everything you ever imagined in the 'perfect partner'. They are quick learners and by listening and watching you closely, they will pretend to be that person you've been looking for all your life. They have the same values, standards and principles as you. How could you have been so lucky to have found someone who mirrors you and all your hopes and dreams? It is so easy to fall into the trap of believing that you have met your soulmate.

The narcissist needs people in their life more than other people. They need narcissistic supply, your time and attention. They need your attention and your admiration just as a plant needs water. Without it, they wilt. They are unable to form normal healthy bonds with anyone, but are experts at manipulating you into bonding with them. Nothing about this idealisation phase is real. It's all a sham. The person who you think they are is really an accomplished liar and actor.

This stage may last for weeks, months or maybe even a year, but it WILL pass on to the next stage and you'll be left reeling, wondering what on earth just happened.

Phase 2

Devalue

Devaluation is the opposite of idealisation, used when a person attributes themselves or another person as worthless, or as having exaggerated negative qualities.

A narcissist's attention span is rather limited, and they get bored easily. Once the narcissist believes they've got you where they want you, they will move on to the next phase of the relationship, known as devaluation. This is the phase when you will see an abrupt change in their behaviour. You will see the real person, the empty shell of a human being that is the narcissist. They come to despise their own dependence on you, their supply, and so their devaluation will begin. They've learned a lot about you in the idealisation phase. When you thought that they were hanging on your every word, they were doing so for a very good reason. They will use every piece of that information, embellish it with lies and use it to discredit your reputation to destroy you. That person who was once so affectionate and loving is now angry and controlling. You may see the narcissist pull away from you and become emotionally distant. You may find you are being constantly criticised, from your appearance to the way you walk, talk or behave and no matter what you do, it will never be good enough. Your feelings of self-worth are slipping so very fast, yet you really can't put your finger on the cause, so you will tolerate more and more of their deteriorating behaviour.

Why do you stay? You stay because you're still holding on to the memories of who you saw in the beginning, the person they pretended to be, and you desperately hope for a return to those good old days. The narcissist is a master of manipulation and deception. They will let you see glimpses of that person they were before just to keep you within their clutches. This form of intermittent reinforcement and then punishment develops into the most powerful of emotional bonds and attachments that are so very, very difficult to sever.

Phase 3

Discard

The discard phase may be described as the getting rid of someone who is no longer useful or desirable, casting aside, rejecting or disposing of someone.

By this time your self-worth is somewhere in the gutter, you may have been isolated from everyone you once held dear because the narcissist managed to convince you they were no good for you. Close friendships are long gone because the narcissist created friction where once there was none. They have succeeded in bringing your self-esteem down to the level of their own. It is at this time that they need a boost, need their ego stroked with fresh supply. You are no longer useful.

They often vanish from your life without warning, initiate one of their infamous silent treatments, no goodbyes, no closure, nothing, zero, zilch. This type of behaviour is known as 'Ghosting'.

In some cases, the narcissist will initiate what they see as inevitable, their own abandonment. Their behaviour becomes so despicable and intolerable that no one in their right mind would want to be around them any longer. Yes, you've had enough, enough of their mind games, their rages and their silent treatments, their lies and their anger. You know when to call, 'Time'.

When that final curtain falls, you will be crushed to your very core, even if you were the one to call time. Nothing you could have done could have changed things. Nothing you could have done could have altered the outcome. Nothing can alter their dysfunction. Making some sort of sense of their dysfunction is not something normal human beings can fathom. Their dysfunction is not your burden to carry. This is the way the story ends each time, until this dysfunctional dance starts all over again...

THE PULL AND PUSH IN A RELATIONSHIP WITH A NARCISSIST

The Returning Boomerang

A relationship with a narcissist can be likened to a returning boomerang, 'a weapon designed to return to the thrower'.

The narcissist's relationships follow a pattern where they pull you into their web with their apparent charm, wit, kindness and generosity only to sabotage it all for no obvious reason. Then, when all seems lost, they switch on the charm again, draw you back into their web and things return to those initial stages where everything is perfect once again...TEMPORARILY.

A narcissist will take you to a point where you to believe that all is lost and when you desperately fight for your survival, they offer a glimmer of hope that maybe, just maybe, it's not the end. You'll grab whatever is on offer with both hands whilst they are revelling in their power over you in the knowledge that you will take whatever you can get, and so the games go on. You convince yourself that things will be better this time.

These sick and twisted mind games are highly effective methods of manipulation and mind control. They play with your feelings and emotions. Why? To feed their never-ending need for narcissistic supply and to get a reaction from you, positive or negative. The way they feel about themselves dictates how they treat you. Whether you deserve it or not is not on their agenda.

'Don't let faded memories of a time long gone take you down that wrong road again. You know where it leads and you know where it ends. It's gonna take you right back to where you've been.'

THE CYCLE OF MIND CONTROL

Narcissists don't 'do' solitude. They need company like a car needs fuel. They thrive on narcissistic supply, good or bad, positive or negative, and cannot function properly without it.

The person who got you hooked once before will again switch on the charm and return to that amusing, generous, even kind person you originally thought they were. You are feeling so confused, maybe you were wrong before, maybe it was all your fault, so you fall for their charms once again. They promise you the world. It's too good to be true! Sadly, it's not. It's not real.

DEVALUATION

The narcissist will get bored again. All the positive supply and adoration is wearing thin. It's not enough. You're not doing enough. It's certainly not their fault and it never is. They blame you. You need to suffer for not giving them the adoration and attention that they believe they deserve. They will shout or fire insults in your direction to provoke you, to hurt you, to get you to beg them, to plead with them. If you should happen to let them see those tears as they roll down your cheeks, they'll be moved, moved to the point of total satisfaction. You may even be subjected to their favourite weapon, the silent treatment. You don't deserve their acknowledgement. Their silence is justifiable. As you plead for an explanation, want to know what you've done wrong and promise to do whatever it is to put it right, their fragile ego is given a much-needed boost. They'll keep up this behaviour for just long enough, long enough to teach you a lesson and pray for their return, but short enough so that they won't lose you, not just yet!!

And now you'll go back to the beginning. They'll switch on the charm and you're back in the web, relieved that once again you're back where you should be. Everything will be perfect for a while... Until the next time.

The to-ing and fro-ing between being treated well and being treated badly over a period of months or years wreaks havoc with your emotions. A state of confusion doesn't even come close in describing how you feel. This goes beyond bewilderment as to why this is happening. And yes, the narcissist is loving every minute. They planned this from the outset. They are masters of manipulation, practising their tactics in every relationship. If the narcissist has done their job well, you may find yourself with no one to turn to, no friends, no family, they have isolated you from everyone you held dear.

If this toxic individual believes that you have figured them out and it's not quite the right time to let you go, they will do everything to keep you from going.

- They may promise to change... They won't.

- They may offer to seek help... They don't need help, they're perfect the way they are.

- They say that it will never happen again... It will.

- They may apologise... It's not sincere.

These are all desperate measures to keep you from leaving. You are not at liberty to decide when the relationship ends. That's their prerogative.

Eventually you will decide you've had enough of the control and the mind games and you'll leave the narcissist, or they will abandon you in the most callous manner that you can ever imagine. Either way, it's not the end.

Don't fall for their attempts to resurrect the past. It's futile. Protect yourself, protect your heart. The outcome has already been decided.

You set the standards of how you will let people treat you. Don't let people jump in and out of your life and treat you with disrespect. Set your standards high and keep them there.

Never run back to the one who almost brought you down.

'Never let your feelings for someone blind you from seeing them for who they really are. Someone who loves you will never get any sort of pleasure from seeing you hurt and knowing they are the cause of your pain. Love doesn't work that way.'

The game a narcissist plays can be likened to a game of tug-of war. It takes two people pulling in opposite directions to keep the game going. When you set the rope down, the game's over. Know when to lay down the rope.

CHAPTER 7

MIRRORING

Mirroring is imitating or copying someone else's characteristics, behaviour and mannerisms.

We have all heard the saying, 'Imitation is the highest form of flattery', and sometimes, in small doses, it is.

In the early stages of a relationship with a narcissist they may mirror your behaviour.
They reflect back to you your very own behaviour and mannerisms, likes and dislikes, morals and values. You very quickly conclude that this person is so very like you. What a coincidence, or is it?

They do this deliberately to draw you in. They will claim to like the same type of food, the same restaurants, they shop in the same shops as you do, they even have the same hobbies as you. It is so difficult today to meet someone who has so much in common with you. It's hard to believe that you two are so alike in so many ways.

Unfortunately, this type of manipulation is a very effective tool in the narcissist's toolbox. Be alert. He or she may be just too perfect!

Sadly, the target of narcissistic abuse may imitate the behaviour of the narcissist to be accepted and valued by the narcissist. Nothing you ever do will please this type of dysfunctional human being. Don't stoop to their level.

MANIPULATIVE BEHAVIOUR

'Manipulative, abusive, controlling people and the weak people who are afraid of them, their enablers and flying monkeys who blindly follow them… will say and do almost anything to keep you quiet. You are going to get labelled as crazy, angry, jealous and hateful, to name but a few, when you stand up to them and call them out on their behaviour. Be strong. You can handle this. The truth is always revealed to those who have learned to see.'

Let's look at what is meant by manipulative behaviour;

Psychological manipulation can be described as exercising unscrupulous control or influence and emotional exploitation over a person or situation with the intention of gaining power and control at the expense of their target. A world-renowned expert on manipulators, Dr George K. Simon has cited three necessities to successfully manipulate someone:

1. Concealing aggressive behaviour and intention.

2. Understanding the psychological shortcomings of a victim in order to determine which method will achieve the best results.

3. An uncommon degree of ruthlessness, having no reservations about inflicting harm upon their unsuspecting victim.

Who do they target? Anyone can be a target of an emotional manipulator.

- Empathetic, kind and easy-going people who try to avoid conflict. These kind and considerate people are likely to forgive the narcissist time and time again for their monstrous behaviour.

- The independent, accomplished person will be a great source of narcissistic supply once they have fallen under their spell.

The narcissist has mastered the art of deception. Although their intentions may initially appear to be honest and sincere, their ultimate goal is to deceive, exploit and manipulate. Whatever the relationship with the manipulator, be it parent, spouse, partner, sibling, child, friend or co-worker, this relationship is unbalanced from the beginning. Their aim is to, by any devious means necessary, gain control of your mind, resulting in you becoming an unwilling participant in their schemes. How can any such connection not be doomed from the outset?

As discussed earlier in the book, narcissists are known to be very observant at the start of any relationship. They listen intently as you reveal details of your past, your feelings and vulnerabilities, to use this information against you for their own gain.

Narcissists are adept at distorting the truth. Manipulators are often compulsive and pathological liars. They will twist events, things you've said or done, turn them around, and maybe add a few lies so that their version becomes a far cry from reality. Of course, their target is left feeling confused and full of self-doubt.

Manipulative people will often play the victim to circumstances they have created. They lack accountability for their words or actions and twist the situation round to blame you.

A common form of manipulation is that of turning people against each other, creating jealousy and disharmony. They talk behind backs spreading false information so that people become distrustful of one another. Splitting, as this is sometimes called, puts the narcissist in a position of power.

Passive aggressive behaviour is common. They go between being pleasant one minute to refusing communication the next (the silent treatment). Their target is left reeling, wondering what they have done wrong when in fact, the answer is, absolutely nothing at all.

Explosive rages and personal attacks and criticism are another favourite tactic. They are relentless in their pursuit of grinding you down until they get what they want. Your emotional health and well-being are of little importance.

Targets of such insidious manipulation unintentionally give up a part of themselves to keep the peace and please someone who is simply impossible to please. Unfortunately, once these twisted individuals succeed in taking advantage of your kind and forgiving nature, they are likely to repeat this behaviour over and over again until you put a stop to it once and for all.

We all have the right to be treated with respect and set boundaries as to what is acceptable behaviour and what is not. Learn to be assertive. You have the right to your own opinions and values and the right to express these without being put down by someone whose moral values are sub-standard to say the least. Never be afraid to say, 'No', and don't feel guilty for doing so.

Remember that someone who feels the need to manipulate others has failed to mature emotionally. Although they may appear to be strong and in control, there are often underlying insecurities and self-doubt. What you see is not what you get. Their dysfunctional behaviour is likely to tumble over from one relationship to the next. They absolve themselves from any responsibility in their continual failed relationships. Narcissists' failure to hold themselves accountable for their behaviour is in complete contrast to them holding you accountable for yours.

- Do you feel you are constantly walking on egg shells around this person?

- Do you feel as good about yourself as you once did?

- Do you feel taken for granted?

- Do you feel that whatever you do, it's never enough?

- Is it always you who is doing the giving and them the taking?

- Are you losing friends, acquaintances without knowing why?

- Are you subjected to their passive aggressive behaviour?

- Does this person try to tell you how you should think or feel?

- Do you feel that it is all about their needs whilst yours don't matter?

- Do you feel pressured into doing things that you are not happy with?

If you have answered 'Yes' to some of these questions, it may be time to re-evaluate what part, if any, you want this person to play in your life.

'Make today be the last day that you care about people who have shown you that they don't.'

GASLIGHTING

The term Gaslighting originates from a 1938 play "Gaslight" and its 1944 film adaptation, in which a husband tries to make his wife believe that she is insane by using manipulative tactics.

A narcissist will use a very effective, persistent form of psychological abuse known as gaslighting to gain power and instil confusion and anxiety in their target.

Gaslighting is an insidious process that occurs over a period of time, resulting in the person being gaslighted questioning their own reality and/or sanity. They will no longer feel that they can trust their own judgement and memory. When someone's recollections of events are constantly put in doubt, it is inevitable that they will wonder if their own version of events is indeed correct. Their self-esteem and confidence will plummet, and they will start to believe that they can't function independently, finding it difficult to make decisions. Anyone is susceptible to this form of abuse, which is akin to brainwashing.

How is this achieved?

Snide comments and a little lie here and there will more than likely go unnoticed. As time passes, these will escalate and even the smartest, mentally stable person can fall prey to such manipulative tactics. They will find themselves being reminded of their shortcomings and weaknesses so that they feel there is something wrong with them and they become so grateful to have the narcissist in their life. Lies become the norm so that they have no idea what are lies and what is the truth. When lies are so utterly convincing, they will inevitably doubt their own perceptions.

'If you repeat a lie often enough, it becomes accepted as the truth.'

To add fuel to the fire, the narcissist who is trying to wear you down will throw in a little praise now and then. Now you are more confused. You must have got it wrong. They're not so bad after all. It must be you getting things twisted.

The intermittent put downs and praise increases your anxiety and stress. You're walking on egg shells in an attempt to please, but whatever you do, it's never quite right. They will continue to ridicule you and point out your flaws. You find yourself always on the defensive and apologizing when you've done nothing wrong. In your mind, you must have upset them, so it must be your fault!

Isolation is another one of their ploys. When they have succeeded in isolating you from friends or family through, yes, you've guessed it, more lies, you will feel that you have no one you can trust except the person who you can trust the least, the narcissist. You are insecure and in a weak position, just where they want you, confused and isolated.

The manipulator may relate a story, leaving out certain information. When they convince their target that they told them specific details of which the victim has no recollection, they will start to think that they are losing their memory and their mind.

The gaslighter will question their target's sanity to just about anyone who will listen. If there comes a time in the future when the target should decide to talk to others about the narcissist's abusive tactics, why should anyone believe them when they know that this person is unbalanced and unstable? Remember that the narcissist is such a convincing liar, and often appears to be so very charming in public, that their 'listening ears' find no reason to doubt them. Who do people turn to for the right information? Certainly not the person being gaslighted.

Typically, in this type of relationship, the person who is being manipulated will defend the behaviour of the abusive personality. They often feel embarrassed and ashamed and blame themselves for the narcissist's behaviour. *'If I hadn't done……., he wouldn't have behaved the way he did.'* *'She doesn't really mean it.'*

Once the target recognizes what is happening it is vital for them to understand that they will never stand on safe ground around this person. It is like walking on shifting sand. The narcissist will never take responsibility for their behaviour.

Anyone who has been subjected to this form of abuse will almost certainly need counselling to build themselves back up to who they once were. A strong support system will work wonders. The feelings of self-doubt and low self-esteem will pass.

CHAPTER 8

BAITING

Baiting means to deliberately annoy or taunt someone by saying or doing something in the hope of achieving a negative or emotional response.

A narcissist will bait someone for their own amusement, to relieve boredom or to extract narcissistic supply. Any reaction from you constitutes supply. They will bait or provoke you to gain attention and any reaction from you, good or bad. If they succeed in making you angry, it proves to them that they have power over you. If at first they don't succeed, they may continue to aggravate you until you eventually snap, and they get their desired response.

Remember, the narcissist has learned just about all there is to know about you, your insecurities, your secrets and they know what will upset you. They will use this knowledge to agitate and provoke. Your reaction will give them ammunition to prove just how unstable you are. Their timing has been perfect. Everyone will see your reaction, but no one will have seen or heard what they did to make you react.

At first, their behaviour will appear to you to be unintentional, but, as time passes you'll know, without a doubt, that they intended to hurt and bait you into a response. The narcissist gains sympathy from those who witnessed your outburst. They know they are tormenting you but what a sense of power they have, to be able to control not only your reactions but how others see you. They derive a sick, sadistic pleasure in watching you in distress.

'Abusive people enjoy this framing game. They provoke their chosen target for a reaction, then claim it as evidence of mental instability, evil-mindedness or something else that implies it is the victim who is at fault. Diverting all attention away from his own behaviour, the bully seeks support from others, turning them against his target. It can be devastating for an individual who already is suffering from mistreatment to be blamed, slandered, rejected and isolated as well. The abuser enjoys the sense of power and control he derives from tormenting with impunity, and the positive attention he gets from playing the victim and fishing for sympathy. It is also an effective method of intimidating his target from attempting to speak up and expose the truth.'

Difficult as it may be, try not to give them the response that they are expecting. DO NOT REACT. Take a step back, calm down, walk away, leave their company or hang up the phone. Don't let them see that they have annoyed you. Don't take the bait!

TRIANGULATION

Triangulation can be described as manipulating tactics in which one person will not communicate directly with another person. Instead they will create triangles where they draw in a messenger, a third person to relay information to the second. Another form of triangulation is achieved by pitting two people against each other, usually attained by manufacturing lies and manipulation.

In romantic relationships the narcissist will have you believing that they are the most desired person on the planet. They delude themselves and tell you stories of their desirability. They will surround themselves with their enablers, their ex-partners, and quite likely, your successor. You feel flattered that you are the one who has gained their attention amongst all their admirers.

One of the ways the narcissist manufactures situations in which they appear to be in such high demand is to triangulate. They will create triangles where they will turn people against one another, creating jealousy and rivalry. Creating jealousy and rivalry does two things. Firstly, it brings about feelings of insecurity in the narcissist's partner, who will feel that they may be replaced. As a result, they will try harder to please the narcissist to prevent this from happening. Secondly, the narcissist will gain narcissistic supply when in their deluded mind they feel both desired and in control of this twisted dynamic.

For triangulation to be successful, the narcissist will be in charge of the flow of information. They will let people know what they want them to know, leaving out information which may portray themselves in an unfavourable light.

Triangulation can take place in any type of relationship. In dysfunctional families, children can be pitted against one another by a manipulative parent, or a parent may try to get the support of one of their children against their partner. In normal relationships, drawing a third person into a disagreement can be helpful and beneficial. However, in a dysfunctional relationship, this tends not to be the case. The third party often feels pressured into taking sides. They may be manipulated into becoming part of a conflict that they have no desire to be involved in. This learned behaviour is seen as the norm by a child and is often perpetuated when the child becomes an adult

Pitting people against each other is known as 'Splitting' in psychology. If the narcissist is getting bored in the relationship or believes that their target has sussed them out, they will spread malicious gossip behind the back of the real victim, to tarnish their reputation. This often takes place before the relationship comes to an end. A narcissist will portray themselves as a victim and their target as unbalanced, even crazy and will blame them for the very things that they have done themselves. Sadly, they are often believed by the listening ears who fail to listen to two sides of a story and pass judgement accordingly.

PROJECTION AND BLAME SHIFTING

Psychological projection can be described as a defence strategy people employ to cope with undesirable feelings, motivations or emotions, by attributing these on to another person. A narcissist will denigrate their target in terms that would more fittingly describe themselves. They may describe someone as being dishonest, rude, of low morals and of being hypocritical when they are, in fact, describing how they themselves behave.

By denying their own negative qualities and attributing them to others, the narcissist can absolve themselves of blame, known as blame shifting. Narcissists like to see themselves as faultless and blame those around them for the very things that they do themselves. They will criticize others, distancing themselves and failing to see that the dysfunction is their own. Projection allows the narcissist to justify their unacceptable behaviour. This form of defence mechanism is typically unconscious and distorts reality.

Neurotic projection is generally the most common form of projection, perceiving other people as behaving in ways one unconsciously finds objectionable in themselves. Complimentary projection is assuming that other people see, do and feel things in the same way that you do. Complimentary projection occurs where people assume others can do things as well as they can themselves.

In psychology and narcissism, it could be said that projection is self-protection in relation to the narcissistic personality so that they do not have to face up to their negative qualities.

CHAPTER 9

NARCISSISTIC INJURY

A narcissistic injury is a perceived threat to a narcissist's self-esteem or sense of entitlement.

Narcissistic injury or narcissistic scar/wound as it is sometimes called is a term introduced by psychologist Sigmund Freud in the 1920s.

While some narcissists give the impression of being confident and self-assured, we know that this is a show to hide their deep insecurities. They are constantly on the lookout for slights and are ultra-sensitive to criticism in any shape or form. Criticism on any level will leave them feeling humiliated, degraded and mocked.

NARCISSISTIC RAGE

Narcissistic rage is the term used to describe a narcissist's unwarranted and immature response to a narcissistic injury, disrespect or a perceived threat to their self-esteem or self-worth.

Narcissistic rage falls into two categories:

- Passive aggressive, they withdraw into huffy, sulky behaviour, giving the silent treatment.

- Explosive which may be verbal attacks or outbursts that can quickly escalate into a physical assault.

Explosive:

Their rage seems to come out of nowhere. It doesn't take much to ignite their fuse and provoke an irrational display of rage, which can be likened to a temper tantrum that one would expect to see from a five-year-old child. They lose their self-control and behave like a lunatic. In the narcissist's deluded world, they believe that they should be revered and respected by all those around them. They depend on others more than they would ever like to admit. Anything that they believe challenges their grandiosity will be seen as criticism. It may be as little as a simple disagreement, you not giving them the attention that they feel they deserve or a negative remark, that will give them reason to justify their noxious behaviour. Should you decide to point out to a narcissist their imperfections, they will not take it lightly. By invoking in them an overwhelming sense of shame and failure, which they never wish to address, they will take their revenge by an explosive display of rage. The narcissist is standing on shaky ground, with their fragility a closely guarded secret. In their mind, having threatened to de-stabilize their position, you deserve to be the focus of their wrath.

Hell hath no fury compared to that of a narcissist in a fit of rage.

Some will resort to name-calling to degrade and bring you down. Please remember that the only one being degraded is themselves, with their below the belt insults.

How should one respond to such verbal assaults? The best way to deal with their rage is to simply ignore their ranting and let it fizzle out. Let them know that you will not tolerate their behaviour. It is not advisable to engage with them in a verbal attack in case this would lead the situation to escalate into physical violence.

Narcissists will see their behaviour as justifiable.

'If you hadn't provoked me, I wouldn't have done that.'

It's your fault, I behaved that way.'

No one is responsible for their destructive behaviour but themselves. Don't let someone try to place the blame where it does not belong.

Passive Aggressive:

THE SILENT TREATMENT

The Sound of Silence

'Stonewalling is a persistent refusal to communicate used by manipulators as a controlling strategy. By simply saying and doing nothing, the abusive personality assumes a sense of power over their target by putting themselves in control of 'if and / or when' any conversation will be resumed.'

The silent treatment is a passive aggressive form of emotional abuse. It is employed by narcissistic personalities as a way of expressing their rage. The target is not harmed physically. The silent treatment is one of the narcissist's favourite games of mind control. Those who have never been subjected to this form of abuse will find it difficult to understand the utter devastation caused by what is sometimes known as mental murder. The narcissist will deliberately ignore their target to cause harm, often encouraging others to do the same (ostracism). The person who is being ignored or ostracised is left feeling worthless and invisible, with their self-esteem lying in the gutter.

The narcissist will express their disapproval by shutting down, withdrawing any love or affection, refusing to communicate and denying their target any explanation. Why?

Avoidance, control, disempowerment and/or punishment for some perceived slight that their target is completely unaware of. They know how they are making the other person feel, but in their sick and twisted mind, they believe they deserve it. Their emotional maturity is typical of a five-year-old child who sulks and storms off until they get what they want. The victim often reaches out to the abuser to try to resolve the situation. Their phone calls will go unanswered, their emails or texts will be ignored. All attempts at communication are met with contempt and a deafening silence. This passive aggressive behaviour is usually a repetitive form of emotional abuse which the narcissist will practice time and time again with each episode of silence often lasting a little longer than the one before. This is intentional manipulation which conditions the target for future mind control. They don't know if or when their voice will be heard, and they will once again be graced with a response, or whether some degree of 'normality' will ever be restored.

A narcissist will assume that you have learned your lesson when they decide to resume contact with you, expecting you to receive them with open arms. For your sake, don't go there.

Below are some questions I put to a narcissist regarding the silent treatment:

Q. Why would you, as a narcissist, invoke the silent treatment on a partner or loved one?

A. They've brought it on themselves. If they have stopped making me the centre of their attention, I can bring the focus back to me by ignoring them. They'll be so hurt and annoyed that they're being ignored that they'll grovel and beg and do anything to get my attention. If they've done something that annoys me, it's a good way of pulling them back into line.

Q. Back into line... That statement certainly makes it sound like you think that you should always be in charge, that you should always hold the reins. Is there ever a time when you can see someone as your equal?

A. No. I am the boss. If they want to be with me, they need to know that.

Q. The silent treatment has been described as mental murder due to the severe emotional trauma felt by the victim. How can you justify making someone feel totally worthless, as if they don't matter?

A. It doesn't matter to me how they feel as long as they learn their lesson.

Q. How do you react when your tactics don't go to plan and your target ignores you right back and doesn't come running back to you?

A. That doesn't usually happen.

Q. What if it did? What would you do?

A. If they were worth keeping, I'd bide my time and gradually draw them back to me.

Q. How?

A. By being charming and irresistible again.

Q. Is it something you do a lot?

A. Yes, 'cos it works.

The narcissist is a cold, empty, rather pathetic human being who will show absolutely no remorse or sympathy for the pain and distress that they are causing their victim. To the outside world their behaviour will appear normal. They appear to be in good spirits, calm and in control. No one would ever believe the person they think they know could act in such a cold and callous manner. They often portray themselves as the victim whilst the real victim of this dysfunctional relationship gradually becomes a shell of their former selves. People who they thought were their friends have sided with the abusive personality. They find themselves rejected by not only the narcissist, but by the narcissist's family members, friends or colleagues. It's a very lonely place to be. The real victim withdraws, doesn't know who they can trust anymore, and becomes isolated. Sometimes they'll react and who can blame them? They have been pushed to the edge and they've done nothing wrong. Bam! The narcissist has all the evidence they need. Their victim has just shown everyone how crazy they are. The abuser has gained sympathy and the victim has shown just how 'unbalanced' they really are.

As the victim's mental health slowly deteriorates, the narcissist knows that they could put an end to this needless suffering at any time. They don't. They often enjoy seeing the results of their monstrous behaviour and its profound effects on their helpless victim.

When does the silence come to an end? When the narcissist sees fit. When the target has been punished enough. When they've paid their dues some semblance of normality will return until the next time. The victim is so delighted that the period of silence has been lifted that they don't ask why or what happened. They don't want to invoke the narcissist's wrath, so they let it slide. Each time someone is subjected to this abhorrent treatment, they become less of the person that they once were. Their self-esteem gets pulled down further and further until they are not a patch on the person they once were.

In most cases this type of abuse is covert and is rarely witnessed by anyone outside the loop. It is considered a very dangerous form of abuse which no one should tolerate. If you find yourself being treated in this manner, understand that this is not normal behaviour.
People who play these mind games are mentally unstable, full of self-hate and are incapable of maintaining healthy, loving relationships.

No one deserves to be treated in this manner by any one.

'There was a time when your silence cut me deeper than any knife ever could.
But then, the more you ignored me, the more I realized
That I deserved so much better...
So much better than you could ever give me
Or could ever be.'

THE SILENT TREATMENT V NO CONTACT - WHAT ARE THE DIFFERENCES?

A lot of people tend to think that when we go 'No Contact' with a narcissist, we are behaving in a similar manner as they do when they give us the 'Silent Treatment'. The two are so very different, and are done for very different reasons. We need to look at what motivates someone to initiate the Silent Treatment or No Contact.

The Silent Treatment

When a narcissist gives us the silent treatment they are doing so as a punishment, to invoke fear, obligation, guilt or remorse. Remember that these disordered personalities are all about power and control. It is a means employed by these disordered individuals of showing their displeasure or disapproval. Have you done something to deserve it? Probably not. Most of the time the victim has no idea why they are being treated in this despicable manner. They have done nothing wrong. Any attempt to resolve the situation by discussion is thwarted. Their contempt for you is blatantly obvious. The narcissist's ego is very easily upset. It takes so very little to ignite their fuse. The silent treatment is a passive aggressive form of emotional abuse which has been described by some as mental murder. When you are on the receiving end of the silent treatment your very existence is not recognised by your abuser. They will not speak to you, look at you, answer your phone calls or answer your texts. This makes a target feel that they are dead to their abuser. The narcissist knows exactly what they are doing, they know how this behaviour is making you feel and yes, they may enjoy seeing you suffer. Basically, they just do not care how they make you feel. In their sick and twisted mind, you have upset them, and you deserve it.

No Contact

When we go no contact with an abuser it is done to protect ourselves, to give us time to heal and recover, not to punish or hurt anyone. It is put in place to break the emotional bonds which have formed between you and an abusive personality. These bonds can be very strong and difficult to break. No contact is thought to be the very best way for someone who has been abused to break those attachments, heal and move on with their lives. (When there are children involved, minimal contact is advised. Keep one line of communication open, preferably in writing. If necessary, contact can be maintained through a third party.)

No contact has often been described as removing drugs away from the addict or alcohol from the alcoholic. The narcissist was our drug and when we need to become clean we have got to stay away from them. How long do we keep up this no contact policy? The answer to that question will be different for everyone. No contact should remain in force until the bonds are completely and unequivocally severed. For many, this may last a lifetime. Some alcoholics may be alcohol free for years and just one drink will see them back in their pit of despair. Likewise, with the narcissist, just one conversation, one time letting your guard down, can be enough for you to let the narcissist back into to your life. Make sure you know that you are strong enough before you have any dealings with the narcissist. For many that time will never come. So be it. Losing the narcissist in your life is not a loss, it's a gain. You are gaining freedom. You are gaining strength away from this dysfunctional individual. You are getting your life back. You cannot stop them treating people the way they do but you can stop them treating you in this way.

Know that someone who truly loves you would never want to hurt you, would never want to see you cry or be the cause of those tears. Know when enough is enough. Know when to walk away.

'When you realize what you have been dealing with for so long, the solution becomes clear. This person isn't going to change. No contact ever again is the best way forward to a peaceful life free from their abuse and toxicity. No contact puts you in control. It is you saying, "I've had enough of your bullshit." It is you placing them in eternal quarantine. For those who find no contact impossible, keep communication to an absolute minimum.'

CHAPTER 10

ACCOUNTABILITY

We all know that narcissists behave in ways that defy all the unwritten rules of common decency. They lie. They demean and degrade. They use and abuse. They behave without morality and without remorse. Yet, in the mind of a narcissist, they never do anything wrong.

We all make mistakes in life and the most of us can own up to those mistakes and admit when we are wrong. This is not the case with a narcissist. It will always be someone else's fault. They will never hold themselves accountable for any wrong doing. They are masters of deception and manipulation who will blame anyone around them for anything untoward.

*'There is nothing dishonourable about being wrong.
The only problem is when you can't admit it.'*

Narcissists have not developed a solid sense of self, with their emotional maturity appearing to be stuck somewhere in their childhood. When confronted with their bad behaviour they will behave like a five-year-old, throwing childlike temper tantrums, known as narcissistic rage. Holding themselves accountable is very difficult for someone with fragile self-esteem. A narcissist is not capable of empathy and can't imagine walking in someone else's shoes to see how their actions may affect others. They only see things from their perspective, how it affects them. Nothing else matters.

The harder you try to get this person to take responsibility for their actions, the more toxic the interaction will become. They will use every trick in the book such as gaslighting and projection to make sure they do not have to admit to being at fault.

Remember that this person does not have remorse and no matter how hard you try they are not capable of admitting they are wrong.

They may:

- Deny.

- Say they can't remember.

- Shut down and ignore you.

- Blame someone else.
- Say how terrible a person you are for accusing them.
- Threaten to punish or abandon you if you carry on.
- Blame you for making them behave in the way that they did.
- Turn the conversation away from their behaviour by criticising yours.

People who never hold themselves accountable for their actions will never learn from their mistakes and are destined to repeat them.

THE NARCISSIST AND PATHOLOGICAL LYING

A pathological liar lies compulsively and impulsively without thinking about the consequences.

Pathological lying is likely to occur with people who suffer from certain personality disorders. Narcissists are skilful liars who tell lies to hurt and harm everyone who comes into their lives. They also tell the truth in misleading ways to give others incorrect perspectives. They study the person they hope to take advantage of, looking for signs of weakness. Liars don't care about your feelings and never will. A pathological liar shows no emotion when lying which is why they are so often believed. Many have been known to beat a polygraph.

'There'll come a time when you see them for who they really are…
A phoney, a liar and a loser.
And when that time comes,
Their opinions and even the mention of their name
Won't mean a thing.'

Some scientists believe that narcissists lie to get attention, to make themselves appear more interesting. In fact, some will even tell lies that are self-incriminating. Any attention is better than no attention at all. Some narcissists lie to paint themselves as a victim to gain sympathy.

People with low self-esteem are more likely to resort to pathological lying to make themselves look better than they believe themselves to be.

When caught out in their lies, narcissists often become extremely defensive and try to blame others. They may fabricate more lies to cover up their original lie.

Some react with anger and rage and may retaliate. Sometimes they lie to avoid confrontation.

Pathological liars often have difficulty maintaining consistency in their lives and often cannot sustain healthy relationships and become estranged from their families.

'I've learned many of life's hardest lessons from a few messed-up people.'

CHAPTER 11

THE NARCISSIST'S SMEAR CAMPAIGN

'The Smear campaign is an orchestrated series of lies and misinformation initiated by toxic people as a method of damage control in the event of them being exposed.'

*'They are going to talk about you and you're not going to stop them
And some of what they say about you isn't going to be good.
There will be lies and slander
And there will be those who believe all that shit.
Let them.
People believe what they want to believe.
Some people are going to judge you
And they've never even met you.
Their foolishness doesn't define you.
It defines them.
You know the truth and that's what matters.'*

Narcissists use a calculated (and effective) series of lies and gossip to deliberately bring you down and make themselves look good. Why? There can be many reasons, such as you seeing them for who they really are, as a way to discredit you should you decide to expose them, jealousy, when your relationship is coming to an end, not giving the narcissist enough attention, or a simple disagreement. It doesn't matter to them how close you once were or how loyal a friend or partner you were. It doesn't matter if you are a close relative or a long-suffering spouse, their treatment of you will be the same. As a target of a smear campaign you will often find yourself isolated and/or ostracised by family and people who you once thought of as friends.

'Don't worry about exposing fake people and liars. Give them some time and they'll expose themselves.'

By the time you find out about the back stabbing and betrayal, it's too late, the damage has been done. No one believes you. Your credibility has been undermined and your reputation has been assassinated. The narcissist has painted a dark picture of you and any denials only add fuel to the narcissist's version of events. Unfortunately, people tend to believe what they hear first. They make up their minds and once they have come to their own conclusions, shifting those views can be difficult, if not impossible. The character of people who listen to gossip must be questioned when they judge and form opinions based on tittle tattle.

The narcissist often starts a smear campaign long before a relationship comes to an end. They plan ahead, knowing that none of their relationships end well, so when that time comes, they have already persuaded friends, and anyone who will listen to them, that their target is unstable. They lie, spread malicious gossip and twist the truth in an effort to destroy their victim's character and reputation. Abusers often use other people to do their dirty work for them. They will use third parties to abuse their target. Because this form of abuse is indirect, it results in them looking like an innocent party. The narcissist will find people who will buy into their lies and deceit and willingly play an active role in discrediting you. In their eyes and in the eyes of those who never bother to look too closely, their hands are clean.

Maintaining their image is paramount. They've done this before and are well practised in manipulating and controlling people. Practice makes perfect and sadly they are often believed. Many people buy into a narcissist's lies and deceit and willingly play an active role in discrediting others. Deception comes easy to the narcissist who is an accomplished liar. The end justifies the means.

Smear campaigns are often initiated within the family unit. The narcissist alienates their target from family members once again by lies and gossip. The narcissist recruits family members, who become enablers, to help ostracise their victim.

Anyone who is seen as a threat to a narcissistic personality within the workplace may be considered a target. Simply being more popular than the narcissist is enough to make you a target of a workplace smear campaign. The victim in these circumstances may find themselves being bullied, isolated or ostracised by their work colleagues. They may find themselves being blamed for failures, poor performance or inadequacies, none of which they're guilty of.

'You may hear stories about me. They'll tell you what they want you to know, but they'll leave out what they did. There was a time when I was good to those people, but they don't want you to know that. Do they?'

Make no mistake, the narcissist knows their target is a good person. They know exactly how they are making their target feel by their betrayal. They simply don't care as long as they, themselves, come out of the situation smelling of roses. Some will take great pleasure and feel a sense of power by simply knowing that they are the cause of another's pain and emotional distress. By their manipulation, they are in control of their target's emotions and of their relationships with others. They display absolutely no remorse or shame in the psychological harm and trauma that they cause to their victim, unless of course, they are caught.

What can you do about it?

If you have evidence of defamation of character through false accusations, seek legal advice. Libel is a published false statement that is damaging to a person's reputation; a written defamation. Slander is the action or crime of making a false spoken statement damaging to a person's reputation.

THE BYSTANDER IS AN ENABLER

'In the end, we will remember not the words of our enemies, but the silence of our friends.'
Martin Luther King Jr

'You may choose to look the other way, but you can never again say that you did not know.'
William Wilberforce

An enabler can be described as person who enables another to achieve an end, especially one who enables another to persist in destructive behaviour by providing excuses, concealing bad behaviour or helping an individual avoid the consequences of their behaviour.

How many people do you know who see something happening which they know is wrong and do absolutely nothing about it?

Have you seen people who know that abuse is taking place and rather then get involved, they turn and look the other way?

Enablers fall into two categories, those who know that abuse is taking place and fail to do anything to prevent it, and those who have been sucked into the narcissist's deception and do not see what is happening. Those in the first category are undoubtedly guilty of being accomplices when it comes to the pain and suffering being endured by the unfortunate target of narcissistic abuse. Those in the second category may not be as culpable. They may not be in control of their own lives. They may be bonded to or have been brainwashed by the narcissistic individual.

It is the first of these two categories that I want to take a closer look at – the person who witnesses others being slandered and abused and fails or refuses to take any action. Enablers are often motivated by self-interest. Their failure to act and take a stand at obvious wrongdoing allows evil to spread its wings and continue. Remaining neutral does not remove responsibility. Their inaction indicates a weakness of character. Good people need to stand up and be counted. They need to stand together and let the abusers and evildoers know that their behaviour will not be tolerated.

'What we allow will continue.'

By doing nothing, the wrong doer will not face the natural consequences of their actions or words. Research has shown that a disordered individual will not see the need for change unless they hit rock bottom. When enablers pander to the abuser's every whim and do not call them out on their behaviour, the abuser will never get to that place where they know that they have got to do something about their monstrous behaviour. Inaction of good people will enable these toxic individuals to keep on doing what they are doing. Narcissists depend on these weak-willed individuals achieve their goals. The pressure to enable may be intense, with the abuser often using manipulation tactics to get their needs met. Don't be fooled and stop making excuses. These 'flying monkeys', as they are sometimes called, need to get a backbone from somewhere, take action and overcome their fear of being the narcissist's next target.

Enablers often rush to clean up the mess left by a relative or friend whose anger has boiled over. Are they helping? Definitely not. Leave the evidence intact. Let them clean up after themselves. When they have calmed sufficiently, let them see how their actions and behaviour have affected others.

'Short term pain vs long term misery.'

Unfortunately, many abusers are not aware of their own mental state and their need of professional help and therefore have no compulsion to receive it. Enabling shields the person from awareness of the harm that they do.

'The narcissist's fan club will change over and over as people come and go. The lifespan of a flying monkey in the narcissist's world is often limited. It's a mug's game. They are expendable and will be replaced when they can no longer be controlled or manipulated or when they are of no further use.'

As we know, the narcissist is on a never-ending search for narcissistic supply. Where this supply comes from, is of little or no interest to them. Vulnerable or weak people often find themselves unable to stop facilitating a disordered person. They remain bonded with this toxic person, finding those bonds impossible to sever. Of course, there will be other loyal little soldiers who will do anything to please the narcissist, to serve their own questionable agenda.

CHAPTER 12

NARCISSISM IN FAMILIES

Unfortunately, not every family is a healthy environment in which to grow or to expect and receive love, respect and understanding. For some people family life can be likened to combat zone from which they see no escape.

The narcissistic family is one that may look ideal from the outside, the family everyone admires. That's how it's got to look. Narcissistic parents want the perfect children from the perfect family but how can any child reach those impossible standards? These disturbed adults want others to be envious of their model family life.

'Narcissists are more concerned about impressing people outside the home than impressing those who live within.'

Dysfunctional families have secrets. What takes place outside the home is a far cry from family life within. There may be endless drama and conflict with children growing up thinking that this is normal in every family. They haven't known any different. In some cases, family is simply the sharing of bloodlines without the healthy components such as love, nurturing and respect. There will be those within the family unit whose goal is to tear you down to make themselves feel good.

THE NARCISSISTIC PARENT

Through our lives we will meet selfish, arrogant, angry and inconsiderate people. We can't change them, but we can decide what part, if any, they play in our lives. Unfortunately, children of narcissists do not have that opportunity.

The narcissistic parent may have what they see as an ideal relationship with their young child. It is certainly the impression that they want to give to the outside world. Their ultimate goal and idea of an ideal relationship is one of total power and control. They write the rule book and the children will comply. The children are seen as a reflection of how they, themselves, wish to be seen. It's each child's duty to make mum and dad feel proud and to set a shining example to outsiders of the perfect child from the perfect family. Nothing is further from the truth.

The narcissistic parent will more than likely have an adverse effect on their children. Their children often grow up without knowing what it feels like to be nurtured and loved in a normal way by a normal loving parent. The controlling parent will ignore their child's personal boundaries, influencing, manipulating and shaping them into being exactly what they want them to be. However, it is not an easy task to fulfil a narcissistic parent's expectations. Children look toward mum and dad to learn behaviour, attitudes, moral principles, emotional attachment and how to treat others. The narcissistic parent's example is not a good one.

As the child grows, the controlling parent may feel threatened by their son or daughter's developing independence. The narcissist has a desperate desire to be 'needed' and hates what they see as their loss of control, sometimes turning against their children as a result.

There are some narcissistic parents who have no interest in their children at any age. They see their children as nothing more than a burden and a hindrance. Their children's feelings and emotions are ignored, with the children being told they are overly sensitive if they complain. They will ignore their children's very existence behind closed doors, where only the members of the dysfunctional family will see the reality of their family life.

The narcissistic parent is difficult to please. Regardless of their children's achievements, nothing is ever quite good enough. Some children will be constantly criticized, teased and berated with their words and actions being disguised as matters of interest and concern. Comparing their child's successes with those of their siblings is a subtle put down by which they minimize their son or daughter's achievements.

There are always exceptions to the rule. Some narcissists are known to treat each of their children in a different manner (favouritism). Some will have what is known as a 'golden child', who can do no wrong, who will be encouraged to do well and be given the best of everything. The narcissistic parent will celebrate even their most minor achievements, whilst their faults and failings are swept under the carpet. This child may receive special treatment for being the perfect child and doing everything that their parent wishes. At the opposite end of the spectrum there is the scapegoat child who will get blamed for just about everything that goes wrong within the family. They cannot do anything right and their achievements, no matter how great, are ignored or dismissed. The scapegoat child is left in no doubt that they do not mean as much to the narcissistic parent as the golden child.

Most normal, healthy parents want their children to succeed in life. However, the narcissistic parent may hold unreasonable expectations way beyond their son's or daughter's capabilities. Their children's success is a positive reflection on them as a parent.

Common Characteristics of Narcissistic Parents:

- The world revolves around them.
- Has unreasonable demands or expectations.
- Is controlling and demeaning.
- Use unnecessary and unjustified criticism.
- Never acknowledges your achievements.
- Compares one child to another.
- Makes you feel like a failure.
- Treats individual children in a different manner.
- Blames the child when things go wrong.
- Is easily offended.
- Withholds love and attention.
- Teaches their children that their opinions don't matter.
- Threatens to withdraw financial support if their needs are not met.
- Threatens to leave you out of their will.
- Disregards your wants and needs.
- Causes friction and rivalry between children.
- Refuses to recognise your growing independence.

Sadly, children of narcissists often grow up carrying the burdens that their parents have bestowed on them. They may have been pushed into the background during their formative years so that mum or dad could take centre stage. They may have been subjected to seemingly endless displays of parental rage. As a result of their traumatic upbringing, children of narcissistic parents often display low self-esteem, having been constantly blamed and put down by their parent or parents.

Some may bottle up their anger, being unable to express their feelings. They have spent all their childhood trying to please their parent and often grow into people pleasers who do everything to please others. People pleasers often pay too high a price; the cost being their own wants and needs placed on the back burner. As a child of a narcissistic parent, they were never allowed to stand up for themselves, resulting in a strong likelihood that this will continue into their adult lives.

It may be necessary to protect not only yourself, but your children, from your narcissistic parent. It may be that you feel that you can never leave your child on their own in the company of your parent. The disordered parent may endeavour to turn your own child against you. Supervised visits may be the only answer. It takes a great deal of strength to stand up to a parent but sometimes you will be left with no choice. You may feel like you have drawn every bad card in the deck when you realize one of your parents may be a narcissist. Depending on the severity of the abuse, the answer may be to spend less time with the controlling parent. Every situation is different. It is not being selfish to value yourself and your needs and to do what is necessary for you to grow into and be the person who you are meant to be.

Some children of narcissists have spent their entire lives trying to please and trying to improve their relationship with their parent or parents only to be rebuked, shamed and put down. When all these attempts have been exhausted, the last resort may be to sever contact with family all together. This can be a heart breaking but necessary decision for your own well-being.

Don't feel guilty and be influenced by others outside the loop who do not understand your position. Your parent may have fooled people on the outside into believing that they are a pillar of society, but you know the truth. Do what is right for you in your own circumstances.

Don't believe the parent who tries to convince you that you aren't good enough. You are. Unfortunately, many will never recognize that it is they are the problem and not you.

Some signs you may be suffering from the effects of childhood emotional abuse...

- You find yourself apologising when you haven't done anything wrong.

- You're sensitive to any form of criticism.

- You cut yourself off from people, preferring to isolate yourself.

- You suffer from self-doubt.
- You don't stand up for yourself.
- You fear abandonment.
- You become a people pleaser.
- You have problematic adult relationships, fear of attachment.
- You feel anxious, constantly on edge.
- You blame yourself when things go wrong.
- You suffer from low self-esteem.
- You bottle up your anger.

HOW DO YOU DEAL WITH THE DEATH OF A NARCISSISTIC PARENT?

Everyone will deal with the death of their controlling parent in a different way. I don't believe that there is a right or wrong way to grieve.

Some will feel angry and hurt. Some will feel regret that they never had a proper loving and supportive relationship with their parent. Some will feel sad that they never shared the good times and now they will never get the chance.

Others will be relieved and that's ok. After years of suffering at the hands of your controlling parent, it's ok to feel numb. It's ok not to cry. You may feel that they died a long, long time ago. You may feel that you lost them a little more each day as time passed and there was no contact. There was nothing left to lose. You have done your grieving before they died and there is no more grieving left to do.

Some people find that the funeral will give them the closure that they never had. Others will not want to attend the funeral and listen to people talking about how sad their death has been and what a lovely person they were. There may be people at the funeral who only saw the nice side of your mum or dad. They never saw what you saw.

You must do what is right for you. Don't let anyone condemn you for your decision. It is your decision. People are often very judgemental when they don't know the whole story. Ignore their opinions. Most people will have no idea how you are feeling. You didn't lose a loving mother or father. You lost someone who could have made you feel valued, loved and supported but chose not to. You lost someone who was never there to dry your tears or wash them away. Their problems were projected onto you. Their problems were there long before you came along so never blame yourself. They could have played things differently but chose not to.

THE NARCISSISTIC SIBLING

Some people think that because you have the same parents and share the same DNA, children will grow into adults who demonstrate similar characteristics and have the same values, morals and behaviour. Unfortunately, children from dysfunctional family backgrounds grow and develop with a completely different view of the world, depending on which position they held within the household.

We have looked at how the narcissistic parent may treat each child in the family in a different manner. Many children grow up believing that they were the black sheep of the family. Maybe in reality they were the white sheep living within a family of black sheep.

If there are two or more children in a family, one of those children is often seen by the parents as the 'golden child' who can do no wrong. The parent sees this child as a reflection of themselves and places high expectations on this child to do well at school and to excel at sports and hobbies. The golden child often develops the same characteristics as their controlling parent. They were not corrected or chastised by their doting parents when they were growing up, so they grow up believing that they are never wrong and that their behaviour is acceptable. They may become egotistical, expect everything their way and have no regard for your feelings.

The black sheep is the child who is blamed for everything that goes wrong within the family and can find themselves being blamed even when they do something well (doing something well paints a different picture and shows you are not as bad as the narcissistic parent makes you out to be). The black sheep are the scapegoat, blamed not just by their parents but also by their siblings. As a young child, this is a really difficult place to be. You may have been taunted and goaded by your brother or sister but somehow it was always your fault. The guilty party always feigned innocence and of course, they were believed. You feel you can never do anything right no matter how hard you try. No one seems to care whether you do well at school or sports. In your mind, you don't really matter, nobody cares. The scapegoat child often suffers deep pain and confusion progressing into adulthood with a very low opinion of themselves. Sadly, such low self-esteem may lead them into developing relationships with controlling people in their adult lives. Being treated poorly has always been the norm.

If you can overcome the negative feelings about yourself, you will realise being the black sheep in the family may not be so bad after all. You are not locked in that narcissistic dance with a narcissistic parent. You are free to do what you want with your life. On the other hand, the golden child is taken by the hand and pushed in a particular direction, always trying to please their narcissistic parent. They will never be free to choose as you are.

Jealousy between siblings is common in dysfunctional families. It is created by the controlling parent who knows that by treating their children differently, friction is likely to occur. Jealousy brings about division and rivalry within the family, with the golden child often bullying the scapegoat child.

Sadly, this jealousy is likely to continue into adulthood, with the entitled, golden child, continuing to bully and berate their sibling. Being the cherished child, they will grow up believing that they should inherit the family assets. After all, they continued to please their parents all their lives, whereas you, the black sheep, were always such a disappointment to them, so why should you deserve anything from their estate? There are no depths too low, to which they will not stoop to get their hands on the family gold.

We can't change people and we can't change how we are treated by our parents or siblings, but we can choose whether we accept their behaviour. As adults we can choose to walk our own path and if that means distancing ourselves from certain people, that may be the direction we will have to take for a peaceful and stress-free life. Most children grow up believing they owe their parents a debt. In healthy families, that may be the case, but where keeping contact with a toxic parent or parents affects your health and your sanity, no or minimal contact may be the only answer. We all have to make the decision based on our own family circumstances. Sometimes minimal contact can work with the implementation of strong boundaries.

'A narcissist will manipulate, criticize, emotionally abuse and invalidate you. Then when you've had enough and stand up for yourself, they'll turn it all around and blame you.'

THE NARCISSISTIC ADULT SON OR DAUGHTER

As a parent, I know of no greater love than the love that a normal healthy parent feels for their children. Children are known to throw the odd temper tantrum when as youngsters they are not getting their own way. We expect that as the child matures and enters adult life, the childish tantrums, pouts and rages will disappear, and the young person will realise that those childish behaviour patterns are not becoming to a healthy normal adult. Sadly, all too often, this is not the case. Some grow into adults who show time and time again that they have no respect for their parents. Nothing the parent does is ever good enough. Some believe the world owes them a living. They threaten to withhold contact with grandchildren unless their ever-increasing demands are met. How do you deal with this type of toxicity when this person is someone you have brought into this world?

Many parents blame themselves, thinking that it must be their fault that their offspring has grown into such an evil and toxic human being. However, this may or may not be the case. Remember that the cause of NPD is uncertain.

No matter how well-meaning your intentions are, your kindness, attention, compassion, forgiving nature, none of it is ever going to be good enough. Narcissistic adult children have an endless list of people who they believe have done them wrong, treated them unfairly, not loved them enough and sadly you are probably at the top of that list.

They hold within themselves a fragile self-esteem and a profound fear of abandonment. They won't acknowledge their fears and their subsequent rages will remind you of those childhood temper tantrums. Do you give in to this childish behaviour and give them what they want? I believe that giving in to their demands will simply invite more of the same. They will blame you for their behaviour. It's a result of what you did or didn't do when they were a child. You will start to believe them and think that your parenting skills were somehow lacking. Don't be blackmailed or held to ransom by their behaviour. They are adults now and need to learn accountability. They are no longer your responsibility.

By ignoring their bad behaviour and giving in to their constant demands, you are acting as an enabler. Don't let them mistake your kindness and compassion for weakness. To do so will result in them pushing you to your limit. You cannot cure them with your love no matter how strong that love may be. I have seen parents who cut contact for short periods of time, only for a return of the same disrespect and toxic behaviour as soon as there is some sort of reconciliation. Some parents want a peaceful life and think that they will achieve it by giving in to the demands of these 'adult kids'. They won't.

I've heard parents say:

"I'm used to it."

"He's done it all his life."

"She's always treated me like that."

"That's just the way he is."

It's time to stop giving in and giving them what they want. Let them know that you are not going to put up with their toxic behaviour any longer. Let them know that it is not acceptable for them to trample over your feelings and behave badly. It's ok for you to demand respect. It's your right. Stop breaking your own heart by giving in to them. You are not doing them any favours in the long run because their obnoxious behaviour, overstepping boundaries, tantrums and rages are not going to stop with you. They will spill over into every relationship they encounter in the future. You, as a parent, are not responsible for their life choices or the consequences of their toxic behaviour.

Whether that means spending less time with someone, loving a family member from a distance, letting go entirely, or temporarily removing yourself from a situation that feels painful – you have every right to leave and create some healthy space for yourself.

Cutting contact with a son or daughter is probably one of the most heart-breaking decisions any parent will face, but sometimes we have to love people from a distance.

Spending less time with your adult son or daughter may be an option worth considering in the hope that some semblance of normality may result. Temporarily removing yourself from hostility may improve the prospects of a healthier relationship when contact is resumed.

Unfortunately severing contact completely is the only answer to those parents who have exhausted every other option. A parent is entitled to demand civility and respect from their children. Sometimes the road to a peaceful life comes at a high cost.

CO-PARENTING WITH A NARCISSIST

Divorcing or separating from someone who you once thought you would spend your life with is never easy. We give up on our dreams, the happy ever after kind of dreams. If there are children involved, two normal healthy adults will seek to co-operate and co-parent and give their children a happy, loving childhood free from disharmony and bitter squabbles between their parents. I'm not sure that there is such a term as co-parenting when it comes to a split with a narcissistic partner. Some would call it counter parenting. Cooperation, compromise and teamwork are not part of the narcissist's vocabulary, so don't expect them to play fair. The narcissist is not going to put the needs of their children before their own. Their maternal or paternal instincts are not normal by any stretch of the imagination.

If you walked away from a dysfunctional relationship with a narcissist, they will not want to lose you as a source of supply. They will not want to lose control over you and one way of maintaining that control is through your children. When children are involved in a break-up it is impossible to go 'no contact' with the narcissist and they know it! The presence of children will force you to keep contact with your ex for many years after the ink has dried on your divorce papers.

It is difficult to understand but your narcissistic ex doesn't love your children like you do. In fact, they may not love them at all. They may simply be seen as pawns to be manipulated, little people who can be used to hurt you. The narcissist may manipulate your children's thoughts. They may lie to the children to turn them against you. When a narcissist experiences loss such as a divorce, they will experience a narcissistic injury or wound and will often react by making the other parent look bad. If they believe that you have wronged them, they will seek revenge by hurting you in the most painful manner possible, alienating you from your children. Children are easily influenced by this covert manipulation.

We know that narcissists love to push you to your limits and create chaos in the lives of those around them. Just because you are no longer together, don't expect this behaviour to stop. In fact, it may escalate. If they can rile you enough so that you react, they can prove just how unbalanced and crazy you are. So, for your own sake, keep calm, don't react and never give them that pleasure.

If you are trying to maintain a semblance of control over your independence, expect a counterattack from your ex-partner. They will not take kindly to your new-found freedom and may try every trick in the book to draw you back into their sphere of influence, such as switching on the charm, looking for your sympathy, threats or hostility.

Since no contact is not an option, minimal communication is advised. Keep contact in writing by text or email where possible, keep it short and to the point. Firstly, this will give you time to think what you are going to say, and your words cannot be twisted when they are there in black and white. Secondly, it leaves a paper trail that may be used as evidence if necessary. Try not to discuss topics about anything other than your children and don't give out any unnecessary information about yourself. If they go off on a rant, disengage and ignore them. Whatever is going on in your life now is absolutely none of their concern.

It is important to set boundaries and stick to them. For example, when your ex is picking up your child, they have no reason to come in to your home. If there are set times for them to see the children, don't let them chop and change arrangements for no valid reason. They may be doing so simply to annoy you, to make you change your plans or provoke a negative reaction from you. Remember that negative attention is still attention to the narcissist.

Hard as it may be, try not to run your ex-partner down in front of your children. As they grow and become adults, they will form their own opinions about their narcissistic parent. Let them do that without any help from you. That way they can't blame you for turning them against their other parent.

Difficulties that may arise when co-parenting with a narcissist may include:

- Telling your child things about you, whether true or false, in the hope of turning the child against you.

- Refusing to pay child maintenance. Narcissists want the very best for themselves. Their children are secondary. The children's needs will not be as important as their own.

- Making you feel guilty if you refuse them more time with your child.

They will appear to be the ideal parent in public. Remember it's all about appearances. I once heard a narcissist described as a street angel and a home devil. To be seen as the perfect parent is paramount. Once again, this is not about the child but how they look to others.

Unfortunately, the behaviour of the narcissist is not likely to change. During this toxic union, you probably felt under their control and always tried to please. Remember that now you are no longer in the grasp of their clutches. You are your own boss. You have control of what you will accept and how you will react. You have the power to keep this person at a distance and not put up with their nonsense any longer.
For your own sanity:

- Keep communication to an absolute minimum.

- Document everything.

- Keep strict boundaries and don't let the narcissist cross them.

- Have faith in yourself, your strengths and your parenting skills.

- Accept that you have no control over your ex's parenting. (Unless of course you have evidence of abuse.)

- Ignore your ex's threats and don't rise to baiting.

Focus on the needs of your children and show them how a loving parent behaves. Over time the narcissist will see that their behaviour is not getting the results they desire. They can no longer push your buttons. Without the attention they so crave, with any luck they will eventually seek their supply elsewhere.

PROTECTING YOUR CHILDREN FROM A NARCISSISTIC PARENT

There is no doubt that narcissistic parents have a detrimental effect on their children's emotional and psychological health. The more you can do to help them through their formative years, the better for their future well-being.

Stop blaming yourself for not seeing sooner the type of personality that you are dealing with. That will not help you or your children. What is done is done and there is absolutely no way that any of their dysfunction is your fault. That burden is not yours to carry.

What you can do now is be a strong support for your children as they mature. You can set an example as to how a normal loving parent should behave. Narcissists will not take responsibility for anything untoward and shifting blame on to their children is not beyond the realm of possibility. Your children need validation, they need reassurance that their thoughts and opinions matter. When a narcissistic parent treats a child unfairly, it is important for the child to know that this treatment is not acceptable and that they are justified and perfectly within their rights to show feelings of hurt, annoyance and anger and that they, at no time, deserved to be treated in such a manner.

Be honest at all times, but be selective. Children of tender years will not be able to understand or accept that their other parent may be a narcissist. Younger children may understand if they are told that their mother or father is easily upset and doesn't like criticism. As they mature, they will see for themselves how their parent behaves and form their own opinions as to their behaviour. As hard as it may be and as tempting as it may be, try not to portray your partner or ex-partner as wicked and evil. Keep those thoughts to yourself for the time being. The time will come when they are older and you can talk to them more openly.

The best you can do for your children for now is to:

- Let them know that they can trust you.
- Show them unconditional love.
- Let them see how someone with empathy behaves.
- Let them express their opinions and emotions.
- Show them that they are only responsible for their own behaviour, not anyone else's.

You may sometimes have to bear the brunt of your children's fears and anger. They know that they can't be honest with their narcissistic parent, for fear of upsetting them, so they will take their frustrations out on you. It is a difficult position to be in, but it should pass. It is also important to ensure that your children do not go overboard with using you as their verbal 'punching bag'. Don't be afraid to let them know what is acceptable and what is not.

It is normal for young children to be selfish but as they develop they should come to understand the needs and feelings of other people. This self-centeredness should diminish as the child matures. Healthy young adults should display empathy for other people and they should be able to understand opposing points of view. Failure to empathize is a warning sign of a possibility of developing a personality disorder.

Medical professionals are reluctant to diagnose anyone with a personality disorder before they have reached the age of 18. However, there are some signs you can look out for if you think they are heading in that direction.

- Threatening behaviour.
- Bullying.
- Making fun of others.
- Showing pleasure at another's pain.
- Constant need to win.

- Thinks they are better than others.
- Reacts with hostility to criticism.
- Violent behaviour.
- Angry reaction to being wronged.
- Blames others for their own mistakes.
- Entitlement issues.

WHAT CAN YOU DO IF YOUR CHILD BEHAVES IN THIS MANNER?

Show your child the value of characteristics such as honesty and compassion. Teach them to empathize. Let them know that kindness and empathy are to be admired, rather than qualities such as greed and entitlement. Ensure that you do not go over the top when it comes to praise. Do give them praise but only when praise is due. Help them build healthy self-esteem. Don't allow them to get away with blaming others for things that they have done themselves (*What you allow will continue*).

There are certain parenting styles believed to promote narcissism in later life such as:

- Neglect.
- Abuse.
- Over indulging.
- Authoritarian attitudes.
- Placing more importance on winning rather than taking part.
- Insisting on perfection.

Young adults can learn to recognise narcissistic behaviour and be taught that this type of behaviour is unacceptable.

WHAT HAPPENS WHEN YOUR KIDS TURN AGAINST YOU?

You have dealt with the frosty stares from people who you barely knew. You've dealt with your so called 'friends' turning against you. You didn't think things could get any worse, but they do. Your own children have been manipulated and they believe all the lies from your ex-partner. The fact that the children have not sided with you will make people jump to the conclusion that you are the abuser and your ex-partner's hands are clean, just as they always said.

Try to remain resolute. Let your children see the strong person you are, not the weak person that you may feel like inside. They don't need to see that. You do not need anyone's approval, not even the approval of your children. You know the truth even if your kids fail to see it. You can't force them to see things from your perspective. Tell them the truth but don't go on about it. If they don't see it now, hopefully they will see in the future that you were the one they should have trusted all along.

CHAPTER 13

NARCISSISM / MOBBING IN THE WORKPLACE

Narcissists don't think that normal rules of decency and morality apply to them. In the workplace, they have no qualms about intimidating and harassing their employees or co-workers and making their lives miserable. Taking credit for another's work, blaming others for their own mistakes, outbursts of rage, jealousy when other workers are better and smarter than they are themselves, are all commonplace.

Narcissists pretend well. They often appear to be charming and considerate but it's the covert put downs and subtle digs that often go unnoticed by many.

If a narcissist is in a job that they cannot do very well, they will resent their co-workers who can do the job so much better and these feelings will give the narcissist a valid reason to target them.

The target person being bullied may feel intimidated, offended and unjustifiably criticized. Sadly, there is rarely any co-worker who will jeopardise their own position to come to their defence. The workplace bully abuses their co-workers, motivated by their own insecurities and selfishness. Their desire to succeed is foremost in their minds. To achieve their goal, they will trample on anyone who they see as competition.

Bullying in the workplace can take many different forms, such as:

- Discrediting someone's reputation with lies and gossip.

- Sabotaging a colleague's work.

- Isolation/ostracism.

- Refusing to answer their telephone calls or emails.

- Regularly undermining a colleague.

- Failure to provide the necessary information, equipment, or tools for the task in hand.

- Withholding important information such as deadlines, meetings and social gatherings.

- Threats of job loss.

- Being rude and talking down to colleagues.

- Stealing and then accusing others of the theft.

- Denying your right to training or promotion.

- Verbal abuse.

- Unfair treatment.

- Reacting to criticism with denial and blame shifting.

- Moves on to a new target once their present target has left.

Mobbing is an insidious form of psychological abuse committed by a group of people and has devastating consequences. Studies have proven that people in a group will behave in a manner that they would never do alone. Normal common decency is cast aside and someone who was once a valued member of a group is shunned and ostracised. The person is excluded from work meetings, social events and their very presence is not recognised. They are often falsely accused of wrongdoing and find themselves the subject of gossip and slander. People find themselves being attacked by their co-workers, superiors and subordinates. Over a period of time, possibly weeks or months, this form of abuse will chip away at someone's dignity and self-respect.

We must remember that human nature dictates that we have an inherent need to belong. Although the scars left by this form of abuse are not visible, they are long lasting and more painful than physical wounds. Long term ostracism often results in alienation, low self-esteem, depression and physical illness.

Shunning is an act of aggression which can have deadly consequences on the target. There will be those in the workplace setting who may not take an active role in bullying a target, but they cannot shirk responsibility for their inaction. Their failure to take a stand, their lack of integrity and their inaction has enabled the abuse to continue. The longer their behaviour continues, the harder it is to bring it to an end.

Suggestions for those who are being bullied or harassed in the workplace:

If the problems cannot be sorted out informally talk to...

1. Management

2. Human Resources (HR) department

3. Trade union representative

If harassment continues most countries provide legal action through employment tribunals.

It is not advisable to turn to your abusers for their approval. Choose to be in the company of people with morals and integrity, people who have whatever it takes to stand up against the crowd, to stand up for honesty and human decency.

Abuse is often directed at one specific target and may go unnoticed by management and colleagues. In some cases, management may be at the helm of the abuse in an effort to force the target to resign. If so, seek legal recourse.

When things go wrong, don't expect the narcissist to accept the blame. It's not going to happen. It's got to be someone else's fault. You may think because you are efficient at your job and have great results, that the narcissistic boss will be thankful. They won't. It's a reflection on them, you work for them and they trained you to do the job. Your outstanding contribution will all be down to them so don't waste your time trying to convince them otherwise.

Don't be fooled into becoming 'friends' with the narcissistic boss or co-worker. Their view on friendship is totally different from a normal person's understanding of what friendship really is. If they are being friendly, it is because they want something from you. If you are of no use to them, they don't want your friendship. Don't go down that route.

The narcissist boss will obtain narcissistic supply by denying their workers their entitlements. Don't expect them to abide by rules or regulations. Normal rules and regulations don't apply to them.

A good boss will have respect for their workers and should quickly notice if there is someone been bullied in the workplace.

Possible signs of bullying may include:

- A drop in the standard of an employee's work for no obvious reason.

- Long term sick leave due to stress.

- Employee seeking early retirement.

- Succession of people leaving employment unexpectedly.

Some employers will not acknowledge that there is a problem in the workforce and fail to address it as they should, and may even try to conceal it. They should note that a happy workforce is a productive one and that failing to address bullying may have a profound effect on the business.

There's a big difference between a firm hand and an iron fist. Employees can be motivated by being valued and encouraged, rather than through fear. This is what separates the good boss from the bad.

Regrettably, the workplace bully often succeeds in their aim of getting rid of their target. The person being bullied will become weary of constant abuse, likely resign and move on. The abuser, having achieved their goal, will set their sights on their next target and repeat the process all over again.

THE FEMALE NARCISSIST

The Toxic Queen Bee

How many people do we meet who want to be the Queen Bee? They are not happy until they have all the attention, with all the worker bees buzzing around after them. Sometimes they can be hard to spot, just like the beekeeper inspecting a frame, as they climb over the worker bees if necessary to get to where they want to be. Young queens quickly seek out other queen rivals and kill them by stinging. Ring any bells? As many as 21 young virgin queens have been counted in a single large swarm. They will fight to the death until only one remains. Unlike the worker bees, the queen's sting is not barbed, and she can sting again and again without dying. The queen bee is surrounded by worker bees who meet her every need.

In life we see people who want to be just like that queen bee. She doesn't care who she stings on her mission to be queen. She will lie, slander, manipulate and trample on anyone who dares to get in her way. She has no compassion, no empathy and will not hold herself accountable for her destructive behaviour.

There will be plenty of worker bees swarming around to assist her on her mission. These people have no backbone. They have no integrity. They have not got what it takes to stand up and say, 'No. This is not right.' They are like sheep, running after each other. Where one goes, they all go.

These controlling people need to be pulled up on their behaviour. The worker bees need to stop buzzing around blindly because their working life is short. What happens when the queen bee no longer needs them? When they are of no further use, they die. People need to stop being cowards and stand up for what is right and develop a mind of their own. They need to stop turning a blind eye. So many people fear being left on their own, being the only one who speaks out against injustice and wrongdoing. Be prepared to stand alone, if that's what it takes. Be brave, stand up, stand tall, look the world in the eye and stop following that crowd that's going in the wrong direction.

NARCISSISM AND FRIENDSHIP

Is a narcissist capable of being a true friend?

Friendship is built upon trust, loyalty, empathy and mutual respect. Narcissists do not possess any of these qualities and as such do not make meaningful friendships. The narcissist does not need friends. They need narcissistic supply. Any so called 'friends' are seen simply as a source of that supply. Acquaintances tend to come and go throughout the narcissist's life.

As with any relationship with a narcissist, 'friendship' with these individuals often gets off to an excellent start. People are impressed and fooled by their charm and charisma. Unknown to them, they are manipulated and used for a time until the narcissist no longer sees them as a good source of supply. At such times these so-called friends are devalued and discarded.

As time passes, people, even those who have hung around for years, eventually see the narcissist's true colours, and how they treat others. If they have not yet been abandoned by the narcissist, they become sickened by their behaviour, by their moods, their continuous conflicts, by their complete disregard for other people's feelings, by their delight at ripping people off and putting others down, that they eventually do the abandoning and leave the narcissist to drown in their own cesspool, which they, themselves, have created.

Time has a wonderful way of revealing truth. The narcissist's social circle vanishes. They are no longer tolerated by those who realise that there is absolutely nothing to gain from holding on to ties with this toxic personality.

Will the narcissist blame others for the situation that they find themselves in? More than likely. They have alienated everyone who has had the misfortune to walk into their lives but somehow, they fail to see that their abandonment has been their own doing.

'A narcissist doesn't like anyone to burst their bubble. Expect a backlash when you destroy their delusions of who they really are. They will try to ruin your reputation by any means at their disposal. Remember, your character is who you are. Your reputation is who others think you are. And don't forget that the wolf doesn't worry about the opinions of sheep!'

THE NARCISSIST IN COURT

If you find yourself in a court case against a narcissist, be prepared for the battle of your life. The narcissist wants to win, by any underhanded means available. Remember that these people are pathological liars and can put on an Oscar winning performance in the courtroom. The narcissist will be one of the most venomous, dangerous opponents one can face in any court of law.

The types of cases you may find yourself involved in are:

- Criminal proceedings where you are the victim of a crime committed by the narcissist.

- Divorce proceedings, where property/money are in issue.

- Custody cases involving children.

- Proceedings involving the return of property/money owed.

If the case is one of divorce, the narcissist will present himself or herself as confident and calm, whereas the downtrodden ex-partner will have been run into the ground by this ruthless individual in the months and years leading up to the court case, and often will come across as stressed and lacking confidence. Do not engage in conversation and avoid any eye contact with the narcissist in or outside the court. If there is somewhere private to sit outside the court, find it, so that the narcissist and any of their enablers are not able to intimidate or unnerve you.

Many people facing a narcissist in court worry that the narcissist will manipulate the court and their lies will be believed. It is vital to ensure that your chosen legal representative is up to speed on NPD. A lawyer who is not knowledgeable is likely to be manipulated by the narcissist and may advise you to settle when it is not in your best interests to do so.

The narcissist has pushed you to your limits in the past. Now it's your turn. Narcissists are likely to react with fury when caught out on their lies and bad behaviour and reveal information which they had no intention of revealing. Their rage may become uncontrollable, with their lawyer doing all in their power to keep them cool, calm and collected (a rather difficult if not impossible task).

The narcissist is likely to have hidden or diverted assets. It is possible to break a narcissist in court, but one needs to be well prepared. It is critical that you are armed with irrefutable, undeniable and corroborated evidence. Avoid giving the narcissist any credible alternative scenarios to the facts. A well-versed lawyer can pose questions to the narcissist in such a way that will take the wind out of their sails ever so subtly.

'I am led to believe you are quite knowledgeable. Sorry, what is your highest academic qualification? ...So, you have no formal qualifications, you never studied for a degree?'

Contradicting or belittling the narcissist's inflated view of themselves will shatter their fragile self-esteem.

Whilst in the confines of the courtroom, position yourself away from the narcissist and never look in their direction. The fact that you are not looking at them will likely cause a narcissistic wound. The narcissist hates to be ignored.

As we know, the narcissist believes they are above the law and not subject to the limitations of the everyday citizen. As far as they are concerned, they outrank anyone in the courtroom including the judge or magistrate. How dare anyone have the audacity to make them accountable for their actions! Anyone who gives evidence against them will be labelled a liar and corrupt.

Never show any reaction to their words or behaviour. They knew how to push your buttons before and they will try it again. Make sure that these attempts are met with indifference.

It can be difficult to relay to the court just how unacceptable the narcissist's behaviour can be. Hopefully, they will supply that information to the court and discredit themselves when their fury erupts in the courtroom.

Always tell the truth. Never be tempted to embellish the truth or paint a false picture. Don't stoop to the narcissist's level.

CHAPTER 14

NARCISSISM AND JEALOUSY

Jealousy is a strong emotion that usually stems from a fear of humiliation or abandonment. The jealous person is in a state of worry and dread, often suspecting a real or imagined threat or a challenge to their possessive instincts.

The degree of pathological jealousy is borne out of deep-rooted feelings of inadequacy, shame and extreme possessiveness. If the narcissist felt good about themselves, they would have no need to harbour such strong feelings of jealousy. Their insecurities will hurt not only themselves, but those closest to them. Due to their lack of ability for self-reflection they are not going to see that their jealousy comes from within, often rearing its ugly head without rhyme or reason. They will constantly be on the lookout for reasons to be jealous, fearing their partner may leave them for someone else.

The narcissist believes that they own another person and that such ownership is necessary to maintain a relationship. Pathological jealousy destroys any relationship bit by bit, often resulting in abuse and violence.

Signs of Pathological Jealousy:

- Being accused of looking at other men or women.

- Being accused of giving too much attention to someone else.

- Checking up on you.

- Laying down rules and regulations by which you should comply.

- Reading personal diaries.

- Isolation, keeping you from associating with others.

- Constantly questioning your activities, who you were with, where you were etc.

- Questioning phone calls or other forms of contact.

- Accusations of affairs.

- Lack of trust.
- Not able to be reassured.
- Blaming you for their jealousy.
- Denies their jealousy though their behaviour is obvious.

Narcissists will encourage feelings of jealousy in their partners as a means of boosting their self-esteem and adding to their partner's feelings of insecurity. To prevent themselves being 'traded in' for another model, their partner tends to try harder to please the narcissist, resulting in further narcissistic supply for the narcissistic personality.

NARCISSISM AND ENVY

Envy is an emotion one feels when one has a strong desire to possess what another person has.

The New Oxford Dictionary defines envy as 'A feeling of discontented or resentful longing aroused by someone else's possessions, qualities, or luck'.

The narcissist is envious of anyone who is better looking, more powerful, of higher status, richer, more successful or more popular than they are. They compare themselves in an unfavourable light to others, but of course they will never admit to such comparisons, for to do so would be akin to admitting that someone else is better than them.

One example of this is the narcissist's envy of the attention you may be getting. If you should find yourself in a situation where you are the centre of attention and not them, their ego is very likely to be undermined.

Narcissists are envious of everyone from their partners or spouses, to their neighbours and co-workers, and even their own children. If their children become successful, the narcissist will have no qualms whatsoever in holding their achievements against them, seething with envy. They will never be happy for your successes and achievements. Don't expect, 'Well done,' or 'Congratulations'. Don't expect them to attend any celebrations. They wouldn't want to be there. If they did happen to turn up they would only try to steal your joy anyway! Their pathological envy stems from their need to be the best in any aspect of their lives. Any threats to their delusional sense of grandeur results in a narcissistic injury. The source of such an injury will be the target of their subsequent rage, aggression and anger.

Some people believe that the narcissist is attracted to weak individuals who they see as an easy target, easy to manipulate and overpower. This is not necessarily the case. A narcissist may initially be attracted to someone who they see as successful or powerful. What a great reflection on themselves to be associated with someone such as this who they can 'show off'. However, as time passes, their envy kicks in and those very qualities they once saw as attractive become threats and something to be destroyed.

Some narcissists will imitate the person who is the object of their envy. They take on their mannerisms and gestures to become just like them.

Signs of pathological envy:

- Undermines your:

    - Achievements
    - Interests
    - Work
    - Friends
    - Reputation
    - Ideas

- Angry if not consulted.

- Unhappy and moody when you receive attention.

- Reacts with passive aggressive behaviour when not receiving the attention they believe they deserve.

- Decides they know best when it comes to what is right for your life.

- Acts depressed when you are happy.

- Starts arguments over your success.

- Shifts the blame and accuses you of their moody behaviour.

Someone who displays these emotions will blame those around them rather than recognising the emotions within themselves that are making them feel hurt and jealous. Only by addressing their self-doubt can these intense feelings of jealousy be quelled. Remember that these jealous individuals only feel good when you feel bad.

NARCISSISTS AND HYPOCRISY

'Do as I say, not as I do.'

A narcissist is a master at blaming others for the very things that they do themselves. They will be quick to point out your flaws, your shortcomings and the negative qualities of those around them but fail to take any notice of their own. They will throw scorn at those who they believe have low morals, yet their own morality, if they have any, leaves a lot to be desired.

Unfortunately, the empathetic soul is quick to absorb blame and accept responsibility when things go wrong. When the narcissist constantly points the finger in your direction and shifts the blame on to you, you start to doubt yourself, thinking that maybe you were at fault. You become a perfectionist, endlessly trying to do things right, trying to please someone who will never be pleased. The narcissist has tuned their manipulation tactics down to a fine art. You are trying to please them, but your efforts will always be in vain, for nothing you ever do will be enough.

NARCISSISM AND SELFISHNESS

In life we will meet many people who we consider to be selfish. They may not be narcissistic, just your average inconsiderate, selfish jerk. Narcissists take selfishness to a whole new level. They will constantly put their own needs and desires before those of anyone else, even their own children. One might say that they are emotionally blind when it comes to the needs and wants of other people. Their selfishness is deep rooted in their disorder. It is part of their character and will affect anyone who is involved with them in any shape or form.

We know that narcissists are self-centred. In fact, we may all be a little self-centred at times and that's ok. It is when this self-indulgent behaviour is the norm that such characteristics are considered unhealthy.

How can you tell if a person is likely to be narcissistic or just plain selfish? Point out their behaviour and see what follows. If you were to point out to someone who is not narcissistic that their behaviour was selfish and rude, how would they respond? I would expect any normal individual to apologise and feel remorseful with undertakings of being more considerate in the future. On the other hand, a narcissist will see your comments as personal criticism, a slight to their fragile ego and would likely respond with either dismissiveness, passive aggressive behaviour or rage. They may turn the situation round and blame you or tell you that you are imagining things. A narcissist will only apologise if it serves their purpose at that moment. However, their apology will not be sincere, and their behaviour won't change.

NARCISSISTS AND THEIR MONEY

Money is power. Money is prestige. Money enables a narcissist to live in a big house, drive the latest luxury cars, wear the best of designer clothes and jewellery, go on exotic holidays and stay in the best hotels. Money makes them look good. Their generosity knows no bounds, at least in public. They may pick up the bar bill and pay for the meal, all for appearances sake. They may complain about it later, but those who they wished to impress will never know.

Narcissists are greedy. They have an insatiable obsession with making money, getting more money, taking control of other people's money, taking your money and inheriting money. They just want more of the stuff! Wealth makes them believe that they are of high status and superior and they look down on those who don't have much. Money replaces all the other important aspects in life, like love and relationships, the very important personal components which are so obviously missing from the narcissistic existence.

Adult children with narcissistic tendencies will do anything to get their hands on the family gold. They will manipulate their parent or parents into believing that they are entitled to inherit all the family wealth. They will lie and convince their parent that their siblings are not worthy of any significant inheritance. They want the lion's share and will stoop to any level to achieve their goal.

If you are unfortunate enough to be in a marriage or partnership with a narcissist who has an unhealthy obsession with money, expect to go without. They control the family budget. They control the purse strings. They will decide how much it costs to run the family home and leave you feeling that you can't buy anything without their prior approval.

Being financially dependent on your narcissistic partner is not a good place to be and they know it. How could you ever decide to leave if you haven't the funds? Keeping you financially dependent on them is a deliberate ploy to keep you from leaving.

Signs of financial control may include:

- Making you account for everything you spend.
- Taking strict control of all finances.
- Insisting family accounts are solely in their name.
- Withholding credit cards and/or money.
- Having to hand over money which you earn.
- Stealing money from you or your family.
- Being secretive over money that they earn.
- Never sharing information about family accounts and finances.
- Not giving you the opportunity to work and earn your own wage.
- Supplying you with a limited allowance.
- Forbidding access to your own money.
- Keep assets in their name, but debts in yours.
- Falsifying accounts and tax returns.

You may notice that although you are restricted to a tight budget, the narcissist can spend whatever they want whenever they want. If you dare to question them on their spending, you will be met with hostility. They are entitled to spend their money as they see fit.

Never doubt that a narcissist who is obsessed with money can bleed you dry and then move onto their next target leaving you financially ruined and in deep in debt.

NARCISSISTS LOVE TO SPOIL SPECIAL OCCASIONS

Maybe it's a holiday you have been planning for some time and the narcissist knows just how much you have been looking forward to the break. Maybe it's a reunion for your closest friends or a special birthday party. Whatever the occasion, the narcissist will do their utmost to make sure that it doesn't turn out to be as special as you had hoped. They want you to share in their own misery.

They don't like to see others happy unless of course, they are the cause of such happiness. Happiness seems so alien to them. Why should you experience joy when they rarely feel fulfilled? Why should they have to put up with being in the company of your friends or family? They are simply jealous of your close friends or the close relationship you have with members of your own family. They know that they haven't and never will have that close bond with anyone. If the celebration is a birthday party or graduation celebration, they don't want someone else receiving all the attention that should be directed towards them. Perhaps if they look dejected, everyone will feel sorry for them and turn their attention where it belongs. The narcissist will do anything in their power to sabotage the occasion.

As your holiday fast approaches, don't be surprised if the narcissist picks a fight with you, and cancels the holiday at the last minute. They may have just found your replacement. Should you find yourself on holiday with a toxic person, and you are doing your best to make the most of your time, they are going to hate to see you enjoying life. They will go all out to ensure that the holiday will go downhill from there on. They will make a condescending remark just to dampen your spirits, or provoke an argument, basically anything to bring your mood down to a similar level as their own.

Whilst on holiday, you may be directing all your attention on making sure the kids have fun. Isn't that what normal parents do? Don't forget this person is far from normal. They want your attention, so they may resort to huffing and bad behaviour to get it. Any attention is better than none.

You want the narcissist to enjoy the holiday or special event, so you try your very best to draw them out of their mood, but no matter how hard you try, nothing seems to work. You feel like they are making you suffer for your efforts to make them smile and be happy. It is like they see you as an enemy, and certainly treat you like one. Only a sick and twisted individual would get some sort of pleasure from ruining holidays and other important events.

What can you do to avoid the narcissist spoiling special events?

Remember that if you are having a good day the narcissist will do anything to spoil it. They want to make the day memorable for all the wrong reasons. Don't give them the opportunity. Let them be miserable, let them drown in their pool of negativity and self-pity. Carry on and leave them to it. Enjoy yourself and let them be. If they happen to come off with some disparaging remark, just respond with something like, 'Fascinating,' or 'Interesting', and go and do your own thing and above all, enjoy the occasion.

NARCISSISTS AND SOCIAL MEDIA

Facebook is a breeding ground for narcissists. They use Facebook, Twitter and other social media because they believe others are interested in what they're doing, and they want others to know what they are doing.

Some narcissists will use social media to get attention. Most people like to keep parts of their lives private and endure illness with a little dignity. When the narcissist is sick or in hospital, don't be surprised to see pictures of them hooked up to drips or machines as they pose for the sympathy vote. They know that by posting pictures of their suffering, they are bound to attract a lot of likes and comments... *'Thinking of you.' 'Hope you're better soon.'*

All comments such as these will give a little boost to their narcissistic supply. If their supply starts to dwindle, don't be surprised if their condition has suddenly deteriorated overnight and yes, more pictures appear of them hooked up to life support.

When a relationship with a narcissist comes to an end, they often post pictures of themselves with their new partner showing the world just how 'happy' they are! Don't believe it. Things haven't changed. They haven't changed. It's just the start of the same old pattern all over again.

Don't be surprised when people who you thought were your friends, stop speaking to you or 'unfriend' you on Facebook. Don't be surprised when people 'block' you on Facebook when they have been manipulated and lied to by the narcissist. Some people will blindly follow the narcissist, listening to just one side of a story and forming their opinion regardless of our side. Let these people go. They have no integrity and haven't got what it takes to stand up for what is right for fear of upsetting and angering the narcissist. Their day will come.

We know that the role of a narcissist's enabler or flying monkey is often short-lived. When they are of no further use to the narcissist, they will realise how foolish they have been when they, themselves, are on the receiving end of the narcissist's wrath.

CHAPTER 15

THE NARCISSIST AND RELIGION

The religious narcissist will see God as perfect, infallible, the all-powerful figure, not unlike how they see themselves.

Beware of the spiritual narcissist who wraps themselves up in the mantle of Godliness. They may go to their place of worship every week and fool the congregation into believing that are a good person with high morals. They can quote scripture and act righteous. They may even be the minister, the pastor or the priest. Being the head of the church, they would have many followers, obedient people who hang on their every word and people who look up to them for guidance. What a wonderful source of narcissistic supply! (*Of course, I am not saying that all people who are preachers or who go to church are narcissistic, but there are some!*) Not everyone who claims to be a follower of The Church, Synagogue or Mosque is a good person.

'Proverbs 4 v 16
For they cannot sleep unless they have done wrong; they are robbed of sleep unless they have made someone stumble.'

The religious narcissist is the greatest of hypocrites, judging others and preaching about fire and brimstone for the wicked and for the unfaithful. Everyone appears to be bound for hell, except them. They use religion for their own ends, to build themselves up whilst tearing others down. If they are your parent you will undoubtedly hear, *'Honour thy father and thy mother'*. Now that's a difficult commandment for anyone to abide by if they have a narcissistic parent.

Narcissists use religion to control and manipulate by inducing fear. Children of narcissistic parents are forbidden to hold their own views on religion. There is no room for differences of opinion. These children often grow up scared witless, fearing death believing they are destined for an eternity in hell.

The spiritual narcissist may:

- Not practice what they preach. (Their behaviour is not likely to match their words.)

- Want to be at the heart of church activities such as prayer meetings and services.

- Display extreme devoutness.

- Put others down by pointing out their shortcomings all in the name of God.

- Think they know the Bible. (Quoting verses from the Bible which back up their views, feigning an excellent knowledge. They will recite verses which point out how right they are and of course, how mistaken you are.)

- Tell you that the Bible teaches you to forgive and forget.

- Make you feel that your opinions aren't worth considering. They are right. You are wrong. There's no happy medium.

Many people stay in toxic relationships because they believe that their religion demands that they should forgive. They have been conditioned to believe that they should turn the other cheek.

Perhaps this verse from the Bible will let people see this logic from another angle.

2 Timothy Ch. 3 v 1-7
But understand this that in the last days there will come times of difficulty. For people will be lovers of self, lovers of money, proud, arrogant, abusive, disobedient to their parents, ungrateful, unholy, heartless, unappeasable, slanderous, without self-control, brutal, not loving good, treacherous, reckless, swollen with conceit, lovers of pleasure rather than lovers of God, having the appearance of Godliness, but denying its power. Avoid such people.'

THE NARCISSIST AND APOLOGY

Some people will say that a narcissist will never apologise. Some won't, but many will apologize if it is in their best interests to do so. They are habitual liars and faking an apology will just be another lie. They don't care how their behaviour has affected you. They will apologise if they have been caught out on their behaviour and an apology will get them off the hook for the time being or if they look good by apologising in public. It is certainly not going to come from the heart. Remember, it's all about appearance.

Will the apology be sincere?
No.
Will the same thing happen again?
More than likely.

When someone is genuinely remorseful, they acknowledge their mistakes, they show and feel regret and maybe offer to put things right, and they try to make sure it never happens again. A major component in an apology is an admission of guilt, an admission to yourself that you have done something wrong or that your actions or words have hurt someone. A narcissist does not like to admit to their guilt and will not hold themselves accountable for any wrong doing. They will use all sorts of excuses to vehemently deny their behaviour or that they hurt you, anything to avoid taking responsibility. Their lack of accountability is astounding.

When a narcissist knows they have acted badly, rather than apologise, they may try to repair the damage by being overly nice and go out of their way to be attentive, or 'buy' your forgiveness with a gift.

Instead of accepting some sort of blame for what they have done wrong, they may try to deflect the blame on to someone else.

'I forgot our anniversary because my brother was sick and I was so worried about him.'

'I'm sorry if you were annoyed, but everyone else thought it was funny.'

'I'm sorry that you thought I said that.'

'I was late getting home because I had to help a friend who was having problems at home.'

'Ok, I acted badly, but it was only because of the way you spoke to me.'

'Sorry for trying.'

These types of excuses may come across as some sort of apology in a roundabout way. The most you can expect is some sort of explanation as to why they did what they did.

An apology from a narcissist should be considered as just another manipulation tactic in the narcissist's game plan or their only way (at the time) of obtaining their much need narcissistic supply. By accepting their apology, you are led to believe that there is good in them after all, and if you were hurt and thinking of leaving, you will get sucked back in and give them another chance, because they are trying after all! What your acceptance of their apology will give them is the green light for more of the same.

What you need from the narcissist is their honest remorse and empathy, but that is something that they can never give you. An apology from a narcissist is for one purpose and one purpose only, to further their own ends. Their words don't mean a thing if they have no intention of improving their behaviour.

THE NARCISSIST HATES BEING IGNORED

Hate them if you want. Just don't ignore them. Ignoring a narcissist is leaving them without narcissistic supply. Attention is attention, good or bad. They would prefer your negative attention to none at all. They need acknowledgement more than anyone else.

If you are ignoring a narcissist they may resort to just about anything to bring your attention back to them. They can't stand being invisible to someone they valued as a good source of supply.

REJECTION AND THE NARCISSIST

Most people find rejection difficult to deal with. If we are rejected by someone we care deeply about, the pain may initially be unbearable, but we accept it, recover and move on, and the pain lessens with the passing of time. Narcissists on the other hand take rejection to the extreme. Rejection and abandonment are two of their biggest fears. They will fight tooth and nail to prevent you from leaving them.

A narcissist is in control and therefore decides when a relationship comes to an end. They certainly do not want to give you that privilege. If you happen to be the one who does the leaving, they know that it was their behaviour that drove you away and as a result will console themselves that they were in control of the demise of the relationship. If they can convince themselves that it was them who ended the relationship, them who did the abandoning, their fragile ego will not receive a blow, a blow that would take them into the depths of despair and depression.

LAUGHING AT A NARCISSIST

Laugh with them but don't dare laugh at them.

It will be perfectly fine for a narcissist to laugh at you, your mistakes and even accidents but it is a different story altogether if you should giggle at their blunders or misfortune. That's where you will find their sense of humour is out the window. Don't ever expect them to be capable of laughing at themselves.

CHAPTER 16

THE AGING NARCISSIST

As a narcissist ages, people eventually see through the false charm and see the person for who they really are. Slowly but surely, the narcissist's social circle dwindles away, one by one people disappear, no longer finding their behaviour acceptable. Most people who have crossed their path in one way or another have borne witness to their deceit and toxicity. Towards the end of their lives there is often not one single living soul who cares whether they live or die. By the time the final curtain falls, they receive what I call poetic justice, getting back what they gave out to others all their lives. As they take their last breath, there's not a hand to hold, everyone who once cared is long gone. Call it Karma, call it God having the final say, call it what you will... I call it pay back.

Aging is a process that none of us look forward to, but it IS better than the alternative. Most of us try to age with grace and dignity, having gained wisdom through the years. A narcissist's behaviour tends to get worse with the passage of time. As time takes its toll on their looks and their health they know that admiration is a thing of the past. Time has taken its toll on their withered frame. They can no longer rely on their outward appearance to attract new supply. They glare at the image staring back at them from the mirror failing to accept the aging face before them. Their mind is not as sharp as it once was. What have they left to look forward to? Retirement? Obscurity? Insignificance? We are always told to look on the inside, look at how someone treats others, look at their heart and look at their soul. It's the inside that counts. What's on the inside of a narcissist? Absolutely nothing but an empty shell. As the years roll by the narcissist faces a complete loss of supply and lashes out at anyone unfortunate enough to be within earshot.

When the Narcissist Is Left Alone

I have a strong belief that people who treat others poorly and have no empathy or compassion for others will be shown no compassion in later life. They have spent their entire lives abusing, betraying and demeaning others, aware of what they do, and without a second thought for the pain that they inflict time and time again. Friends and ex-partners have become enemies. If their children haven't already become strangers, the narcissist may try to buy their children's love in a feeble attempt to keep them close, believing that they may be the only people left on this earth who will put up with their pernicious behaviour. These meagre efforts to be seen as a good parent may be welcomed by a child who has spent a lifetime seeking mum or dad's approval. For others, it will be too little too late.

'An ironic twist of fate…
Their enemy will be their memories.
They can never undo what they've done.
They can't escape their thoughts
When they find themselves alone,
Unloved and abandoned.
When their evil has been uncovered,
The truth will pursue them,
Wherever they go.'

The narcissist is an immature, angry, volatile and controlling individual. They spend their lives attempting to form relationships. Sadly, it's not a partnership they are seeking but a dictatorship where they have all the power and control. Eventually people get sick and tired of their behaviour and abandon them. A string of failed relationships adds to their already fragile ego. By bringing about their own abandonment as a result of their abusive and despicable behaviour, they inflict upon themselves a deep narcissistic injury. Somehow, the narcissist will delude themselves into believing that their own self destruction is someone else's fault.

Much like a drug addict without their supply, the narcissist can't cope when supplies become scarce and runs out. They become chronically depressed and angry and find no pleasure in anything. Their noxious behaviour becomes more demanding and worse by the day. Things that they used to enjoy no longer hold their interest. Their world has become hostile, their social life non-existent. No one wants to be in their company for any length of time. They often become a hermit, closed off from the outside world, blaming everyone else for the situation that they find themselves in. The longer the lack of supply continues, the worse their insecurities and paranoia become.

The narcissist clings desperately to nothing, resenting the passage of time yet helpless to prevent it. They may create fake profiles on social media to stalk people, people that they may never meet or talk to. Surfing the Internet may give them the opportunity to get a little attention from someone, from anyone. They've lost faith in themselves. They don't like themselves and nobody else likes them either, so they think, *'There's no point in being nice.'*

Narcissists have an enormous fear of their own mortality. As death approaches, they know that complete oblivion is on the horizon. Life gives back to them exactly what they deserve, loneliness and isolation. They find themselves being shunned and ignored. The one thing that they never could control is time. As they move forward to eternity they have the knowledge that there is a final judge, and this time, it's not them.

THE NARCISSIST AND ILLNESS

People will say that when they have become ill, the narcissist didn't want to know. They were not interested and basically didn't care. They saw it as your problem, so get on with it. So what happens when a narcissist gets sick? They will milk it for as long as they can. They will take all the sympathy and concern that they can muster, and then some.

They will see their illness as a reason to demand your attention 24/7. Cast any plans you may have aside. Your focus must be on them until they are better. After you have nursed them back to health, taken them to the doctor, collected their medications and tended to their every need, don't expect them to show you how grateful they are for your tender loving care. They aren't. It was your duty after all. You could have done more.

There are times when a narcissist will fake illness, fake a heart attack, fake cancer, in fact fake anything, just to focus attention on themselves. They may do so when you are ill, go one better than you with an illness much worse than yours in order that they get the attention that should be focused on you.

THE NARCISSIST ON THEIR DEATH BED

I am often asked if a narcissist will change when they are on their deathbed. Will they want to put things right and apologize to all those they have hurt in their lifetime? Some people want closure and expect a change of heart from the narcissist as they take their last breath. A deathbed apology is extremely unlikely. They are likely to die the same way that they have lived, hurting others. Many will use this time to twist the knife in just one more time.

Don't beat yourself up if you decide not to pay them one last visit. It is a matter of looking after yourself, a matter of self-protection. There is no point in opening old wounds to satisfy the demands of someone who inflicted those wounds in the first place. If they wanted your company, they should have shown remorse before this late stage, and they should have acted better.

Pity them for being the person they are if you must, but please be careful to never give them the chance to hurt you again.

Death is not always the end. The narcissist knows that their lack of remorse before taking their last breath is going to cause you more agony. Would it have been so difficult for them to have acknowledged the pain they had inflicted on you over the years? Would it have been so difficult to say the word, sorry, one last time and for once, mean it? No. Their cruelty is beyond measure.

The narcissist knows that they can still cause rivalry and division even after their demise. They know that their will may cause rivalry between their children and yes, they may purposefully leave most of their estate to one child, knowing that there will be conflict over who gets what.

The narcissist may be hoping to rest in peace while making sure that peace between their children is impossible, and they are the reason, even in death.

THE NARCISSIST AND SUICIDE

If a narcissist believes that they have reached a point where they may lose you, (and they have no new supply lined up), they won't want you to go just yet. When they have tried everything to get you to stay and nothing seems to have worked, they may threaten suicide as a last resort.

Whether the person threatening suicide would follow through with their threat is not for us to decide. None of us know what is really going through their mind. My view would be to ring the appropriate emergency services and inform them of the situation. Consider if this is something they do on a regular basis when they don't get their way and inform the medical professionals. People who 'attempt suicide' (e.g. by taking an overdose but call emergency services themselves) are often lost souls crying out for help. People who have decided to take their own lives generally do so without warning.

Threatening suicide to make you do something or not do something is emotional abuse. No one should be held to ransom in this way. You are responsible for your own life. If someone else decides to end theirs, you are not responsible. Passing the information on to the appropriate authorities will take responsibility for their actions out of your hands, should they decide to follow through with the threat.

Narcissists are known to use the threat of suicide as a method of manipulation. They have also been known to carry out their threat as an ultimate act of control and vengeance. They know that you will feel guilty and blame yourself. Some will take this act of vengeance to the extreme and take with them those who you love dearly, such as your children or parents.

Of course, not all people who commit suicide are narcissistic. Some may suffer from extreme depression and see no other way out. My husband, Gary, took his own life almost 11 years ago at the age of 56. There was no advanced warning. He would have been the last person that one would have expected to take his own life. He had visited his doctor the previous week with symptoms of depression and was prescribed medication. Sadly, he never gave them a chance to work.

CHAPTER 17

HOW A NARCISSIST LOOKS AT LIFE AND YOU

(From the narcissist's point of view)

When you first become entangled with me, you will always belong to me. You become mine, my property, to do with as I see fit. Your opinions, hopes and dreams are immaterial to me. You need to stop thinking of yourself and put my needs above all else. Give me all your time, attention and admiration or there will be hell to pay. Your hell, not mine.

In the beginning you were the centre of my world. Soon I will be the centre of yours.

You will learn to accept my version of the truth. I will never be responsible when things go wrong, and believe me, they will. It's inevitable. Don't expect me to ever accept blame. It will never be my fault. I don't make mistakes. Instead I will shift the blame on to you every time.

I will manipulate you into thinking the way I do. I will control your mind and your free will, so that you start to think that you no longer have a mind of your own.

You will become so confused that you start to doubt your own reality, your very sanity and the ability to trust yourself will be slowly eroded.

I know who is good for you and who is not. If your friends and family are not on my team, you will be urged, manipulated and eventually forced into discarding them. When you have isolated yourself from your friends and family, you will be completely at my mercy, having only me to turn to for support.

I will read your mind. I know what you are thinking even when you don't know yourself.

I am above the law. Normal rules apply to everyone else, not me. What was once yours now belongs to me. What is mine, is mine. If I want something I will have no qualms in taking it. Borrowing is another word for permanent possession, mine.

I will control your happiness or lack thereof. You will not be happy unless that happiness is brought about by me. I will control your moods so that my shame becomes yours.

Do not set boundaries. I will see those as barriers to be torn down and crossed and I will succeed.

Do not ever question me on where I am going or what I am doing. You have no right to know. Never criticize me for my behaviour. My behaviour is always above reproach. If you can't accept that, then you have no place within my fold.

Whatever you do for me will never be enough. You could have done more or have done better. That's just the way it is and will always be. Don't expect gratitude from me. I will always be dissatisfied with your efforts. When you see my dissatisfaction, you will try harder and harder to please me and do a better job next time. I am pulling your strings and you don't even know it. To see your never-ending struggle to please me amuses me for a time. I deserve special treatment, you can't rise to the challenge and will always fail to meet what was expected.

The goal posts never remain static. They will be moved again and again to meet my unreachable expectations.

I will continually put you down so that you bear no resemblance to who you once were.

If I move on or if you leave me, I will show you how insignificant you were to me, as I move on to someone else as if you never existed.

I reserve the right to come back to you when I see fit. You will receive me with open arms as I come back into your life for a while, as I see fit. Nothing in life is permanent.

If I lose control over you, I will control how other people see you. I will let people know how you hurt me and they will believe me because I have already sowed the seeds.

Never cross me. I will never forget, and I will never forgive. I will get my revenge.

I win, you lose. That's just the way it is.

Remember that you are nothing without me. You need me. I do not need you.

CHAPTER 18

DO NARCISSISTS REALLY LOVE THEMSELVES?

Undoubtedly there are narcissists who truly do believe that they are awesome. They have an unrealistic view of their talents, looks and achievements. This individual displays confidence in themselves and is less likely to be as sensitive as their *vulnerable* counterpart. A grandiose narcissist believes that they are more important and superior to others and view other people with disdain. They believe that they deserve the utmost respect and admiration. They know they are the bee's knees and that's all that matters. If you fail to recognize this, that's your problem, not theirs, and they really won't have much need for you.

Generally, narcissists don't like themselves very much, have very low self-esteem and are constantly on the look-out for proof of their worthiness. This type of narcissist is haunted by fears of rejection and abandonment and hides behind a mask which conceals their deep-seated feelings of insecurity and self-doubt. They are on a continuous quest to overcome these feelings of inadequacy. They will build themselves up by tearing others down.

CAN A NARCISSIST CHANGE?

Can a leopard change its spots? Once we discover the real person, the person behind the deceptive outward appearance, we often wonder if they will change, if they can change.

The subject of change is open to debate. It is a question that has been asked time and time again. It is a difficult question and one that there is no straightforward answer to, but I will give you my answer and please note, this is my own opinion. I believe that generally, no, these people do not change. They don't want to change. They want everyone around them to change. Many professionals in the field of psychology will say that they cannot change, it is their personality, it is their nature, and it is who they are. Change would involve the person with NPD recognising that the problem lies within themselves, and a cure would entail having a conscience and learning to empathise.

Empathy is described by the Cambridge English Dictionary as;

'The ability to share someone else's feelings or experiences by imagining what it would be like to be in that person's situation.'

I don't know about you but from my experience, even if they can imagine what it would feel like to be in another's shoes at a moment in time, they simply don't care. If the negative feelings are not felt by themselves, then the matter is not of their concern.

Our feelings and emotions define our character and define who we are. Emotions in someone with narcissistic personality disorder have not advanced and developed with age as one would expect to see in a normal healthy adult. Their emotional maturity is limited.

If you believe that you are the one person who is going to change them, think again. You can't save a narcissist from themselves. You need to concentrate on saving yourself from the narcissist.

If someone looks at themselves in the mirror and doesn't like what they see, they may resort to cosmetic surgery. Does a narcissist like what they see in the mirror? Most of the time I would think that they do but I don't believe that they take a very close look. They live in denial. They know that if they look too closely, they will see themselves for who they really are. Rather than having their delusional image of superiority shattered, they take a step back from the mirror, not wanting to see what's really there. By having blind spots, they can carry on regardless, fooling themselves that when relationships don't work out for them, it will always be someone else's fault, never their own.

Are there exceptions? Yes, I believe that there are. Everyone in life has their difficult times and we learn to deal with life's problems and move on. What happens to a narcissist when their problems become so overwhelming that they wonder, '*Could this be me?*' '*Could I be the one that has a problem?*' When every relationship that they have in their lives bites the dust, some may have this wake-up moment. Change is an inside job. They need to want to change and sadly the majority never feel the need to change. The road ahead would be a very difficult journey, trying to change who they are, trying to change a lifetime of beliefs and behaviours. Can it be done? If they have reached a point in their lives where they don't like what they see in the mirror, where they have hit rock bottom and when they realise that their strength will come from change and not control, then maybe, but don't count on it. I believe that for those who possess just a few of the traits of NPD, there is a possibility that their behaviour may be modified for a time. Just how long that period of time will last, remains to be seen.

Cognitive Behavioural Therapy has shown a limited amount of success. I have yet to read of a malignant narcissist changing for the better over the long term.

'As you get older you realize that some people are just shitty human beings and there's nothing you can do to change them. If they don't want to change, you can't do it for them. Stop searching for the good in them that simply isn't there.'

At the end of the day, I believe that the likelihood of any significant change is negligible.

Try not to fall for their assurances that they have changed. Assume that they are the same individual that they were in the past. A narcissist can put on a very convincing act in order to persuade you that they are a different person now. If you have managed to move on without this person being a part of your life, don't go back and put yourself through all the pain and hurt once again. Those days are likely to return. A narcissist is likely to remain a narcissist until their dying day.

Does Counselling Work?

Narcissists generally don't do well in therapy. They tend to believe that they are flawless and it's everyone else who has a problem. If they feel that they have been pressured into attending therapy, don't be surprised when they turn it all around and have the therapist and you believing that you are the toxic one. It is tough coming to the conclusion that this person is very unlikely to make any noticeable changes in their behaviour, but facing the truth sooner rather than later may spare you from future anguish and misery.

WHY DO PEOPLE STAY?

So many people stay in relationships of one type or another because of feelings of obligation, for example, obligations felt towards a parent, whilst others stay because of feelings of guilt as to what would happen if they should leave. Many stay because of hope; they keep hoping and waiting for change that sadly rarely comes.

Many people have contacted me who have wasted 30 or 40 years of their lives staying with a spouse in the hope that at some time, their partner would see the error of their ways and they would live happily ever after. None of them ever did.

There are plenty of people who have been hoovered back into relationships with narcissists after believing that the relationship was over, with promises of change. We make excuses for them. We want to believe they've changed and that things will be different this time. Unfortunately, this is rarely the case. Nothing has changed. They are still the same person who they were before, but they can be ever so convincing.

Some stay because they believe that if the narcissist keeps coming back that they must really love them. Sorry, but someone who truly loves you would have never left you in the first place, and would never have wanted to cause you so much pain. Love doesn't work that way.

Some stay because they think that their love and devotion will change a person, hoping that the narcissist will cherish them, since they love them like no one has ever done before. Don't break your own heart. The narcissist will take and take from you until you have nothing left to give and then, and when you are depleted physically and emotionally, they will get their supply from your replacement.

We all have to know when to call time, when enough is enough. We deserve better than these people can ever give.

CHAPTER 19

TRAUMA BONDING

When a 'normal' relationship comes to an end the two parties involved will usually spend some time grieving the demise of the relationship. After some time has elapsed they feel ready to face the world again, fully recovered. However, when it comes to the end of a relationship with a narcissist, the recovery period often takes much longer. The victim (and that's not a word I like to use in these circumstances, but I will do so for clarity), often finds themselves tied to their abuser by some invisible power. No matter what their abuser has done to them, they feel drawn back into their web, as if they are being pulled back into the relationship and they have neither the strength or desire to fight. You may ask, 'Why would someone return to abuse?' The answer to that is a psychological phenomenon known as 'Stockholm Syndrome'.

In August 1973, armed criminals entered a bank in Stockholm, taking four hostages, three women and one man, and holding them for six days. By the end of their ordeal the hostages had surprisingly formed some sort of bond with their captors, defending their behaviour to the police. One later got engaged to one of their captors. Another paid towards the legal fees of one of the hostage takers. Subsequently, this unhealthy attachment between a victim and their captors or abusers became known as Stockholm Syndrome or Trauma Bonding. Patrick Carnes, author of *The Betrayal Bond*, has stated that all these relationships share one thing, they are situations of incredible intensity or importance where there is an exploitation of trust or power.

The vast majority of people who become involved with a narcissistic personality talk about their initial feelings of having met their soulmate. The intensity of the connection produces feelings that may not have been experienced in other relationships. This rollercoaster ride is a never-ending cycle of psychological warfare, where an abuser offers their target kindness and love, bringing them to the edge of utopia, only to take it away or threaten to take it away. When their target is given a glimpse of seventh heaven again, they'll grab it with both hands in the hope things can return to the way they were in the beginning. This cycle of punishment and reward builds very strong emotional bonds. Misplaced loyalty is always associated with some sort of danger or risk.

This unhealthy attachment is strangely the norm as opposed to the exception in relationships with narcissistic personalities. These bonds are difficult to break and tend to become stronger over time. When it comes to severing ties with an abusive personality, the bonds may appear to be unbreakable. The bad behaviour and the lies become acceptable. The victim longs for a continued connection with someone who they know will cause them more pain. They find themselves wanting to be understood by someone who clearly doesn't care. They hold onto secrets and trust people time and time again who have long since proved themselves to be untrustworthy. Regrettably, many people find themselves bonded like glue to the abusive personality, and return to the abuse. Others will never take the step to free themselves, having been totally worn down by the narcissist, holding on to the false belief that they need this harmful person in their life.

Signs of trauma bonding may include:

- Thinking that there is no way out of a relationship.

- Seeing the same pattern of behaviour from the other person, punishment and then reward when you behave.

- You are given the silent treatment when they feel you have done something wrong.

- Unfulfilled promises of a change in their behaviour and you know, deep down, it's not going to happen.

- You want to leave, you are not happy, but something is holding you back.

- If you leave, you feel drawn back into the relationship like a puppet on a string.

These bonds can be broken when there is no contact of any description with the abuser. Some may find it necessary to seek help and support from therapists and/or self-help groups to detach completely.

CHAPTER 20

HOOVERING

The term, 'hoovering' comes from a popular brand of vacuum cleaner. Just as the dust gets sucked up into the cleaner, so does the target of abuse, as they get pulled back into a relationship they are desperately trying to leave or have already left. A narcissist does not want to lose control over you and will make all sorts of promises to draw you back in. There may be promises of change, gifts, compliments and professions of their undying love for you. Be careful. Don't fall for the false promises. I know, it feels good to see the person you fell for a long time ago again. It's good to see them realize that their behaviour has been questionable and are finally owning up to their actions. It's not real. They haven't, and they won't.

A narcissist wants to test you to prove to themselves that they can get their foot in the door again. They may not want to resume a relationship with you, but they need to prove to themselves that they can if they want to. Knowing that you will take them back envelops them with a sense of power. When you show a positive response to a hoover, they may disappear again, in the knowledge that you have not moved on and that they have you exactly where they want you.

When a narcissist realizes that they have pushed you too far, when you start to pull away from or leave the relationship, when you assert your boundaries, they don't want to lose your narcissistic supply. Do remember that narcissists do not like to be alone. If they do not have fresh supply already lined up or if your successor has been discarded, they will want to draw you back into their web. They have manipulated you before. In their mind they can do it again. They will say and do anything that they believe you will fall for. In most cases, their promises and apologies don't mean a thing.

The narcissist doesn't like to lose good sources of supply. They like to think of you as a puppet who can be pulled back into their sphere of influence on demand. They want to hold on to the control they once had over you until your dying day. If you were the one to have left them, they've got a score to settle. They want to prove to themselves that you will take them back and that they are still in control. Once they have achieved their goal, you will most likely be unceremoniously dumped. They control the ending, not you.

I have heard it said that finding yourself in a power struggle with a narcissist is a bit like a game of tug-of-war. If you put down the rope, the game cannot go on. They will either fall flat on their face, urge you to take up the rope again or find someone else to play with. For your own sanity, you've got to know when to put the rope down.

Narcissistic personality disorder is a pattern of deviant behaviour that unfortunately is unlikely to change. They know you are a kind and forgiving soul and they hope that you will forgive them just one more time.

How to you react if you really do believe that they are sincere? What should you do if they agree to counselling?

Keep strong boundaries in place and don't allow them to be crossed. Do not let yourself become isolated. Keep your friends and your family close. Time will always give you an answer. The success of therapy is debatable. If someone is genuine and willing to do whatever is necessary to change their behaviour over the long term, they will be happy to wait and understand your reticence in believing them initially. If the abuser is indeed lying and hoping for reconciliation without a change in their behaviour, they can rarely keep up their façade for lengthy periods of time. Their false promises should reveal themselves soon.

WHY DID THE NARCISSIST NOT COME BACK TO ME?
WHY IS THERE NO HOOVER?

When recovering from a relationship with a narcissistic individual, most people will read up NPD, try to learn all they can about this disorder and try to figure out why they feel so bad about a break up with someone who could treat them so badly. You will read about the narcissist's hoover and expect them to come back at some point. When this doesn't happen many people ask themselves, 'why not?' They take it as an insult that the hoover didn't take place and subsequently question themselves...

'Why didn't they want me back?'

'Was I not as good as the others?'

'They hoovered their other exes back, why not me?'

'I have so much to say. Why won't they hoover me?'

Anyone who hasn't experienced a relationship with a narcissist will think that you need your head examined if you want this person, who you claim has hurt you so much, to get back in touch with you. Don't worry. You're not alone. You need to feel validated. You feel you want to get things off your chest. You have so much to say and you want them to hear it. You want them to know that you've figured them out.

Forget about all that. Be thankful that they haven't. Whatever you have to say to them isn't going to make a difference. They do not care how you feel or the fact that it was them who made you feel the way that you do. Change the way you look at things. A hoover by a narcissist should not be looked at as any form of compliment. It's not. It's all about supply, power and control. Thy want to reel you back in just to prove that they can. I would take it as a compliment if they didn't try. I would look at from a different angle… *They know that they can't fool me again. I know what they are, and I won't go down that road again. I'm stronger now and they know it.*

Now is the time to concentrate on yourself.

There are reasons that you may not have been hoovered such as:

- They know that you have figured them out.

- Fear of exposure.

- Rejection (Fear of you causing a narcissistic wound).

- You may be aware that they have recruited their flying monkeys to gauge how you feel about them.

- You have followed no contact to the letter and they have no way of getting in touch with you.

- They are so involved with your replacement. It's not the right time, just yet.

- Sometimes a hoover will come when you least expect it. They want to control if, where, and when.

Be grateful that you are away from this toxic person and don't be tempted to have a platonic relationship with someone who used to be a romantic partner. All you will be doing is prolonging your pain and your recovery. They weren't a good partner. They are not going to be any better as a friend.

CHAPTER 21

DO YOU WARN THE NARCISSIST'S NEXT TARGET?

Many people want to know if they should warn their ex partner's new target and let them know exactly what they are letting themselves in for. Most kind-hearted people don't want to see others going through the same sort of pain that they, themselves, have endured. They hope that they will be believed when warning the narcissist's new target, and the new target will escape the situation and move on with their life relatively unscathed and forever grateful. Think again.

The consensus of opinion is to leave them to it.

The narcissist is one step ahead, so by the time you find out about their new partner, they have been spreading lies that you are the crazy ex. How you don't want to let them go and will do anything to keep them. By contacting the new partner, you will likely confirm the narcissist's accusations that you are the obsessed, insanely jealous ex. The new target does not want to and will not see the evil that hides behind the fake persona. Instead of driving them apart, you will probably strengthen their relationship. The new partner will sympathise with the narcissist who has endured such a difficult relationship with a psycho!

Let's go back in time to when you first met the narcissist. How would you have reacted to words of warning from one of their previous partners? Would you have believed the words of someone who you believe to be crazy and when all the evidence points to the contrary? We all know that when you first meet a narcissist, they fool you with their charm and charisma. You have no reason to doubt they are not your perfect partner. You're a match made in heaven and nobody is going to tell you otherwise.

Let's not forget that the narcissist is a pathological liar who is well practised in the 'art of lying' and they will, more than likely, be believed. You, on the other hand, will not come out of this situation smelling of roses and will likely suffer further heartache as a result of your good intentions.

It's difficult to think of your ex skipping off happily into the sunset with their new love.

Please remember, it's not going to be a happy ever after scenario. They haven't changed. Their new partner is blinded by rose tinted glasses. They will likely get the same treatment as you did a little down the road, maybe even worse. Now is the time to stop thinking of everyone else and focus on you and your recovery.

SEEKING REVENGE

You want to get even, I know, so your first reaction may be to seek your revenge by lashing out. It's perfectly normal to want to see the person who hurt you to your very core receive a little taste of their own medicine. It's hard to think of them walking off without a care in the world. I know, it might look like they are happy. They certainly want you to think that they are, but remember, this new-found happiness isn't real. It's fake, just as fake as they are. This new addiction will pass, they will soon become bored, and repeat their cycle of abuse all over again with someone else. Be thankful that it's not you.

William Shakespeare was not far wrong when he said, *'The best revenge is to be unlike him who performed the injury.'*

If you want to remain stuck in the narcissist's web of dysfunction and if you want the narcissist to stay in your head and in your life, go ahead and seek your revenge. They are going to love the fact that they still have control over you. They will know that your mind is preoccupied with them even after they have gone. Do you really want to give them the satisfaction? Revenge will prolong negativity in your life. Once you have got your revenge on them, they are going to make you pay, and pay big time. The narcissist will want to make their revenge a hundred times better than whatever you dished out to them so be very careful! The best advice I can give you is to walk away with your head held high. Leave them to create drama with someone else. Leave them to whatever hell they have created for themselves.

The best investment you will ever make is the investment you make in yourself. Dreaming of and wishing for revenge is keeping you stuck in the past. That's not where your future lies. Don't let a narcissist take any more of your life away. They have already taken enough. Focusing on them is letting them have control over you. Don't give them that power. The ball's in your court. You're in control now. Whether you select reverse and go backwards, or you select drive and move forwards is up to you. Make the right decision.

EXPOSING A NARCISSIST

One of the things that a narcissist fears most is being exposed. They have lived their lives fooling people into believing that they are someone completely different to the person they are. The way in which they are perceived by others is extremely important to them. Very few people have borne witness to the real person behind the fake persona.

The reaction you may receive from the narcissist will depend on whether you are calling them out on their behaviour in private or in public. In the first of these two scenarios, don't expect them to accept responsibility. If you are assuming they will see that their behaviour is toxic, think again. They will likely shift the blame and accuse you of being the toxic one.

If you decide to shame them in public, the narcissist will react in one of two ways.

Whether it is safe to expose a narcissist will depend very much on the person you are dealing with.

Some will fade into oblivion never to be seen again, embarrassed and annoyed that people have heard the truth of who they are. If your exposure of them is seen by them as successful, they may move on to new pastures, where their past is not common knowledge, in the hope of starting afresh and finding new targets to abuse.

Others will be angry and see you as an enemy to be annihilated. They will react with rage and may escalate the smear campaign which is likely to be well under way. They will go to any lengths to discredit your version of events, hoping to turn things around, portray themselves as the victim and thereby gain sympathy. Some will resort to verbal aggression whilst others may resort to physical violence. Be mindful and look out for yourself and your safety.

CHAPTER 22

SCAPEGOAT

The scapegoat is someone (or group of people) who is unfairly blamed for the wrongdoings, failures, mistakes and faults of others. For example, a child in a family may be singled out and subjected to unwarranted negative treatment.

The scapegoat is the person chosen to shoulder the blame in a dysfunctional family when things go wrong. It is certainly not an ideal position to hold and sadly often carries with it emotional and psychological damage which may last for many years, if not a lifetime. However, it may be the better position in the long term as the scapegoat or black sheep often escapes the constraints of the dysfunctional family in later life. They can free themselves from the chains which once confined them in childhood.

The scapegoat is chosen for a reason. The narcissist likes to be surrounded by people who are easily manipulated, people who will conform and people who will provide copious amounts of narcissistic supply. The narcissist has figured out that this person, the black sheep, is not going to fit the profile. No, they see strength and they see resistance. They see someone who will not fall for their exploitation. They see someone who has a will of their own and someone who is empathetic. So, if you are the family scapegoat, be proud of yourself. You were a force to be reckoned with. They saw something in you that you didn't and maybe still don't see in yourself…your strength.

COGNITIVE DISSONANCE

Cognitive dissonance is a psychological term which describes the mental discomfort (psychological stress) experienced by a person who simultaneously holds two or more contradictory thoughts, beliefs or values at the same time.

Abuse creates a sense of anxious confusion where a target doesn't trust their own perception of events.

A narcissist will invoke these feelings in their target by denying something that happened or something that has been said, resulting in anxiety and discomfort in their target, who starts to doubt their own reality.

Sometimes people hold very strong beliefs and when they are presented with evidence which opposes those beliefs, they find it impossible to accept evidence to the contrary. Dissonance is often strong when we go against our own moral standards, for example, if someone believes that they are a good person and goes ahead and does something wrong or bad, the feelings of guilt and discomfort are known as cognitive dissonance.

Cognitive Dissonance can be reduced when you receive validation that your recollection of events is, in fact, correct.

RUMINATION

Rumination can be described as a chain of repetitive thoughts which focus your attention on the symptoms of your distress, personal loss, depression and/or anxiety. Instead of focusing on solutions, your focus is drawn to the possible causes and consequences.

People who have been or are in a relationship with a narcissist tend to practice a lot of self-reflection. They may have been constantly blamed when things have gone wrong. They analyse their feelings and their behaviour repeatedly without getting answers. Unfortunately, this negative rumination or worry often leads to depression. Rumination has also been linked to post-traumatic stress disorder, eating disorders and binge-drinking.

Going over and over your problems in your head, instead of focusing on solutions and recovery, is likely to have a detrimental effect on your health and lengthen the period of depression. Dwelling on your sadness, failures and the circumstances around your emotions are going to keep you trapped with negative thoughts. Healthy alternatives to rumination are positive distractions, things that take your mind off your problems.

Rumination is generally considered to be unhealthy. However, there is a time and a place for everything. It can be beneficial and helpful in the right circumstances. Talking over problems with the right people, be it family, friends or therapists, people who understand, can reduce stress when it leads to better understanding and greater insight into the underlying causes of your problems.

CO-DEPENDENCY

The individual characteristics of co-dependency vary from person to person. Some of the more common characteristics would include being subservient and trying to avoid making decisions, preferring to rely on others. Co-dependents are often perfectionists who persistently put the needs of others above their own. This tends to make them feel needed.

Co-dependants often stay in relationships that are emotionally destructive and/or abusive. Enabling is often a sign of co-dependency. They tend to give people too many chances and ignore bad behaviour. They rarely stand up for themselves but if they do, they often feel guilty and distressed.

Unfortunately, co-dependents put up with the narcissist's bad behaviour with grace and composure to keep the relationship ticking over without invoking the narcissist's anger.

EMPATHY... A RARE GIFT

Being an empathetic person means putting oneself in another's shoes, being capable of imagining yourself in their position, and understanding exactly how they feel. Empathetic people don't want to be cruel to others, because they don't want to be the cause of another's pain or suffering. On the other hand, people with narcissistic personality disorder are cold-hearted and show no regard for the needs and desires of others. Narcissists are ultra-sensitive beings who are very easily offended. Their compassion is reserved solely for themselves. They lack empathy and appear to be oblivious as to how their behaviour may make another person feel. It should be noted that a narcissist can fake empathy when required, if it benefits them.

Some may see empathy as a gift, to be able to love from the heart with a love that runs deep, but that kind of love is perhaps open to the deepest of hurt. When you have that extra special gift, it is often exploited by a narcissist resulting in the most unimaginable pain. When you can love someone so much and the love you give is thrown back, the betrayal cuts more than words can ever express. That's the kind of love that only truly empathetic people can fathom. If you are that sort of person, you truly are a rarity in this cruel world we live in today. You are the sort of person the narcissist wants to win over, use and abuse. You will meet their needs, for a time. You love making others feel better about themselves. You want to heal their wounds and make them feel whole again. You want to see the best in people so when you first catch a glimpse of their ruthless behaviour or their extreme selfishness, you will turn a blind eye, believing it was just a one off, believing you can help them become a better person.

Sometimes this world seems so alien to people like you and it is, but would you have it any other way? Would you really want to have a cold heart? Would you swap your caring heart for one of stone, so cold that it can never experience a loving, meaningful relationship of any description? You've got a gift that those cold-hearted people envy. Yes, they're jealous of you. You have got something they want but can never have. You can enjoy life. They can't. You're sensitive, you're kind and you understand. That's something to be proud of because that's something that this world needs more of. You're there if someone wants a shoulder to lean on. You're there if someone needs your compassion, your understanding and above all, your strong sense of loyalty. Yes, that's another rare quality in this world today so don't you ever doubt yourself. You've got that something about you that makes you the person others turn to when they need support, when they need to unburden themselves with their troubles. And being the person you are, you never fail to deliver. That's what makes you a cut above the rest.

Being an empathetic person can sometimes be a lonely place. Because of your kind and forgiving nature, you may be a magnet to a toxic person. They may see you as an easy target, someone who they can manipulate and who will keep on forgiving them when they don't deserve it. You want to help others even when they have shown a dark side of their character, even when they have hurt you to your very core. You feel you can fix those disordered souls who must have been so damaged that they can't feel the love that you are so willing to give. No matter how much you try, they're not going to get it. They're not like you and they never will be. They've not got what you've got. Within the husk that was once their soul, lies a void that can never be filled. Compassion, empathy and love are words that they will read about but will never fully understand. Their emotions are stunted, lost somewhere between their childhood and now; never to develop into the mature feelings that you have been blessed with. Yes, sometimes it hurts like hell to be so caring, to be able to put yourself in someone else's shoes and feel their pain, but that makes you who you are. You've got a heart of gold. By all means, be forgiving, but to a point. Some of us give too many chances, but we've got to know when enough is enough; when to draw the line, and in doing so, we can make sure that it can never be crossed. Don't let your gift be your downfall by giving your everything to those who will give you nothing but pain and heartbreak.

'Stop blaming yourself for taking too long to see just how toxic someone really is. Sometimes we are blinded by what we don't want to see. These people are good at what they do. They are masters of manipulation, lying and shifting blame and placing it where it does not belong. They simply took advantage of your good heart.'

When the relationship ends, and it more than likely will, the empathetic soul can heal and recover. It will take time and a lot of it. The wounds will have cut so very deep. It will be a learning experience and one that you hope will never be repeated. Learning about this disorder and realizing that none of this was your fault will help you on your healing journey. The narcissist will carry on as before, failing to learn anything from each failed relationship. They are destined to follow the same pattern repeatedly, remaining stuck in their misery and unhappiness, never realizing that they are the cause.

THE EMPATH AND THE 'WOUNDED' NARCISSIST

As we know, the cause of NPD is not known, but one of the theories is abuse in childhood (other theories include overvaluing as a child, learned behaviour, and genetics).

Some believe that narcissists have been wounded in their past, that they have been subjected to unimaginable pain/abuse and as a result, they have taken on a certain set of behaviours as a way of dealing with their past. However, many people have been subjected to abuse and yet have found strength within themselves to not let their past dictate their future.

What happens when the 'wounded' narcissist meets an empathetic person?

An empath is a giver who wants to help, being highly sensitive to the needs and feelings of others. They take on another's pain and internalise it. They are full of compassion, believing in the good of humankind. They are able to put themselves in another's shoes and try to make things better, often at the expense of their own wellbeing. On the other hand, the narcissist is a taker, sucking others dry for their own benefit, regardless of the consequences or who may suffer as a result (as long as it's not them). It may be a match made in heaven for the narcissist, but it's a match made in hell for the empath.

Empaths tend to think that people are inherently good, failing to see that there are some people who don't possess such qualities as empathy and kindness. It's hard for them to realise that some people are out for what they can get with no good intentions whatsoever. They may feel themselves being drawn to the narcissist, who has gained their sympathy with the sad 'stories' of their past and how they have been so wronged.

Empaths fail to set boundaries as to what is acceptable and what is not. A narcissist will seize this opportunity to take advantage of their kind and forgiving nature. Their aim will be to exploit and manipulate the empath by any means necessary. The narcissist has mastered the art of deception and will employ well practised, devious and underhanded methods to exert their influence, whereby they will eventually gain control not only of their target's mind but virtually their every move. This type of psychological abuse is a gradual process in which the person being targeted has absolutely no idea that such wheels have been set in motion. Their objective has been to love, to help and to soothe the pain that the narcissist has so convincingly made them believe has been a part of their past.

Let us not forget that narcissists are pathological liars, often portraying themselves as the victim, where the opposite is true, and they are, in fact, the perpetrator.

Can these two personalities find an equilibrium? That is highly unlikely. Over time the target of this insidious abuse will get worn down. Just like a carpet that gets constantly trod on, its once beauty and soft touch are now lacklustre and barren of fibre. They will get fed up with constantly being blamed when things don't run smoothly. Sometimes the empath will start displaying the traits of the narcissist when they see that their needs and wants are never being met. The narcissist won't like this 'change' in their behaviour, seeing it as selfishness. (Of course, they will never see that it is a reflection of their own behaviour.)

They'll get fed up with being the only one fighting for the relationship. Sometimes this process takes years, but eventually most realise that there is a point of no return. It's either sink or swim. As a captain of a ship performs his last duty by ensuring the safety of the passengers and crew before saving himself, the person seeking freedom ensures the safety of their children and loved ones, before jumping overboard and swimming for the shore. Some may think that they can remain on board and hope that the ship will remain afloat, but often the damage is too severe, and sailing on to the sunset is not an option.

Abandoning ship is not failure. It's not defeat. It's taking positive steps to overcome a situation that has become unsustainable. Remaining in an unhealthy relationship with such a toxic personality is likened to signing your own death warrant. Psychological abuse takes its toll on your health, not only your mental health but your physical health. It's not selfish to take over the reins and start looking after yourself. You have a choice, to stay and be subjected to more of the same, or give yourself a new start, a new life free from mind games and control. The choice is yours and the journey ahead will be rough at times but worth it.

For those dealing with family members who display this type of behaviour, the advice from experts is the same. Distance yourself from the dysfunctional personality to gain peace and normality in your life.

CHAPTER 23

NO CONTACT AND DETACHMENT

Detachment is a process, sometimes a very long one, of letting go of someone who we know we will be much better off without. If you have been in any kind of relationship with a narcissist for a lengthy period of time, you will have experienced times where you have doubted your own self-worth. You will have started to believe the narcissist when they have criticized and blamed you when things haven't gone to plan. Now, you have got to the point where you know the problem is not you and it never was.

The love and respect for someone has been replaced by anger and resentment. You know that you deserve so much more than what they can ever give. You know that you don't want to walk on eggshells forever, trying to please someone who will never appreciate all that you do. You know that it's time to call it a day, time to move on to a better life. The only way to ensure that the narcissist can no longer hurt you is to completely detach and refuse to engage with them on any level.

Gone are the days when you will put up with their bullshit. Now it's time to fight back and fight for yourself. You know that you are no longer the weak person that you once thought you were. It's time to think about yourself. It's time to put your needs first for a change and that's not being selfish, it's self-preservation. Put as much distance as possible between you and them.

Once you have got to this point, it's time to put in place a set of rules for your own protection. No contact can be described as a set of rules that you apply to yourself giving you time and space to recover. Keeping any form of contact with an abuser will keep you from moving forward with your life. If you break these self-imposed rules, the person who is going to suffer is you.

Once you have decided to bring an end to the relationship, it is important to tie up all the loose ends such as:

- Returning each other's property.

- Finding separate accommodation.

- If applicable, initiate divorce proceedings.

- If you have mutual friends, let them know. (If they continue to have contact with the narcissist, avoid contact with them for as long as is necessary. If they support the narcissist, let them go.)

- Remove reminders of the narcissist from around your home.

- What exactly will no contact entail?

- Do not text.

- Do not make or receive phone calls (if they ring you from an unknown number, hang up when you hear their voice).

- Do not read or respond to emails.

- Block them on social media.

- Do not snoop on Facebook or other social media (you don't need to know what they are doing or who they are doing it with).

- Do not meet up.

- If you pass them on the street, look the other way.

- Avoid going to places where you might run into them.

- If you happen to work with them, keep to the rules when and where possible. Keep communication on a business level only.

Let the abusive personality know that you are severing contact and ask them not to contact you in any way. They may not respect your decision, but the ball is in your court now. Show no emotion. You are in control. When a narcissist realizes that you are now no longer under their control, they may eventually give up and stop trying to contact you.

If there are children involved or if for some other reason it is impossible to implement no contact, keep contact to an absolute minimum and keep it in writing when and where possible. Keep your conversation restricted to the children.

BOUNDARIES

YOUR LIFE, YOUR RULES

Boundaries have been described as a set of limits or rules which a person decides are reasonable regarding how other people should behave towards them. These conclusions are made based on personal opinions, beliefs, likes, dislikes, upbringing, experiences and social learning. They work in two ways, both inward and outward; how you expect others to interact with you and how you interact with others. It may take time to find the right balance, so that they are neither too weak nor too strong.

Boundaries are an important component in any relationship and may differ from person to person. We've all met the person who just has to invade our personal space and gets a little too close for comfort. Whilst close proximity is acceptable with some people, with others, it's uncomfortable to say the least.

We need to decide what is acceptable in our lives and what is not. Normal, healthy people know not to cross the line. They've got a reasonable idea when not to intrude. Narcissists, on the other hand, don't possess healthy boundaries and have no respect for yours. They don't like you setting boundaries and putting limits on their behaviour. However, they have an uncanny way of pushing you to your limits for their own amusement, to create friction or maybe just to relieve their boredom. Boundaries are all about cooperation, a word which appears to have been omitted from the narcissist's vocabulary. Setting boundaries with a narcissistic personality is not a one-off thing. Expect it to be something you will need to address repeatedly. It is possible to set boundaries with a narcissist, but you will need to stand strong. Communicate your wishes firmly and directly and don't let them push your buttons. Say your piece and walk away or end the conversation if you must, but leave them in no doubt that you mean what you say. Learn to say, 'No', or 'That doesn't suit', and mean it.

Setting parameters is something we should all be doing. First and foremost, it is taking care of yourself, which is an important part of your wellbeing. Never let anyone make you feel guilty for setting your standards. In close relationships, communicating your needs to your partner should not make you feel uncomfortable. If they get angry with you or go against your wishes, they're not giving you the respect that you deserve. They are the one with the problem, not you.

Healthy boundaries include 'alone time' and time to spend as we see fit, with friends and/or family, and we should feel free to keep those relationships alive.

A dysfunctional family background often leads to a child believing that their opinions, needs and desires are meaningless. As they grow up, these children need support to make them understand that they are not insignificant, to help them develop a healthy sense of self and form healthy relationships in adult life, unafraid to set boundaries as to how they should be treated.

Boundaries can be likened to a fence around your home which clearly defines your property. Without those fences confusion will arise. Some people may cross your boundaries from time to time with your consent. And there will be those who disregard them and enter uninvited with harmful intentions. That's when you need to reinforce your boundaries, build a wall and close the gates.

GREY ROCK

As discussed earlier in the book, no contact, where possible, is the best method when dealing with a narcissistic personality. However, there are some situations where no contact is not possible, for example, where children are involved. In these situations, a technique known as Grey Rock can be implemented.

Grey Rock is a method you can employ whereby the narcissist is encouraged to lose all interest in you. When going no contact, all forms of communication are discontinued. Grey Rock differs from no contact in that you don't avoid the narcissist. Instead you keep contact, albeit to a minimum, keeping your responses so utterly boring that the narcissist will see you as a poor source of supply. Your aim is to blend into the background, become insignificant and be as boring as you can possibly be. Talk about the most boring topics you can imagine such as ironing, doing the laundry or how you enjoy watching paint dry. No-one wants to be in the company of boring people and the narcissist is no different.

- Be dull.
- Be monotonous.
- Be tedious.
- Be uninteresting.
- Show no emotion.
- Never stroke their ego.

- Show that nothing new ever happens in your life.

(Never let the narcissist know that you are implementing Grey Rock.)

Don't show any reaction if they try to provoke you. Let the narcissist see you like a well that has run dry as far as narcissistic supply is concerned. As you know, narcissists thrive on drama. Keep your contact with them drama free. They will soon get bored and move on to someone who will be a much better source of supply.

CHAPTER 24

FORGIVENESS...SHOULD WE FORGIVE?

We often read that we should forgive the narcissist so we can be free and move on with our lives. I'm not sure that I agree with this. Forgiveness is a personal thing. It is one thing to forgive someone who shows remorse for their words or behaviour, is genuinely regretful and tries to make amends and change their behaviour. It's a different story altogether when someone intentionally hurts you, even takes great delight in doing so and doesn't give a damn how they make you feel. Narcissists know exactly what they're doing. Why would someone with such evil intent deserve our forgiveness? In their twisted logic, they maintain control and a sense of pride in their despicable behaviour. They may force themselves to apologise for their behaviour if it's to their own advantage, but there will be zero sincerity.

Without any semblance of remorse from someone who has wronged us and hurt us deeply, feelings of bitterness, hatred and sometimes revenge often bubble to the surface even within a person who is generally of a forgiving nature. I believe that in most cases, these feelings will pass in time.

I know that this is such a debatable topic, but when we forgive someone who is not sorry for their behaviour, are we not giving them the green light for more of the same?

I know that many people will say that forgiveness is necessary so that we do not become weighed down by bitterness and hatred. I am often asked if I have forgiven my ex-partner. The answer to that must be no, and to be completely honest, I don't think that I ever will. He doesn't deserve my forgiveness and I know that I am not burdened with bitterness or thoughts of revenge. I am relieved that he is no longer a part of my life. There is a special place in hell for people like this.

I know there will be those who will disagree with me and say that the Bible tells us to forgive and that may be so, but then there are verses such as this one...

Luke 17.3
Take heed to yourselves. If your brother sins against you, rebuke him; and if he repents, forgive him.

I think we all need to do what is right for ourselves. Some people will say that forgiveness does more for the forgiver than the forgiven. I think the jury is out on that one.

CLOSURE

'So many people want closure from a narcissist.
YOU DON'T NEED IT FROM THEM.
Now, what sort of closure can you expect from someone with the emotional maturity of a toddler?
Give it to yourself. Pull down the shutters and bolt every door so that they never open again. Let them toddle off into whatever hell they have created for themselves. You've got your clarity and you know it's better this way. That's your closure.'

When a relationship with a narcissist comes to an end, many people find that they can't move on with their lives until they find closure. Closure is not going to come from the narcissist. It has got to come from yourself. There will be no, *'I'm sorry, I treated you badly'*, or *'I didn't mean to hurt you'*. Narcissists like to think that you will forever be under their influence and control. They don't care if you're struggling and find it difficult to move on without any form of closure from them. They are not going to feel any shred of remorse for the way that they treated you. In fact, it's very likely that they will blame you for the demise of the relationship. You didn't treat them with the respect that they deserved. You didn't give them the attention they craved. By now you probably get the picture. A relationship with a narcissist is not a normal one by any stretch of the imagination and the ending will be no different. That final curtain may fall with such shattering speed that you don't know what's hit you.

Sometimes there will be no rhyme or reason as to why you have been discarded or abandoned and they have moved on so quickly to their next target, as if you never existed. Such a callous discard will have you questioning your self-worth and wondering if you ever meant anything to them at all.

Trying to find an explanation and closure from a narcissist will cause you more pain. They will never see things from your point of view. They are experts at re-writing history.

Finding closure starts with cutting the narcissistic individual out of your life in the form of no contact.

You have got to let go of the thoughts of them being the person you once thought they were. They have shown you their true colours. Don't try to paint a different picture.

Many people, in their desperate struggle to get some form of closure, write, text or email, pleading for answers, only to be met with silence. The narcissist's lack of empathy and compassion will never have been more obvious to you than it is now. They will not be feeling sorry for your anguish, but what they will be doing is relishing in the supply you are providing and their power over you. Your pain will show them just how important and significant they are. For your own well-being and as a matter of holding on to your self-respect, don't pour your heart out to a selfish person whose heart is as cold as ice. Show them that you can do just fine without them. Your indifference will cause them a narcissistic injury, which is what they deserve.

Researching the subject of NPD is a good start. It will help you to understand why they behaved the way that they did, that the problem is not you and that they are destined to repeat this pattern of behaviour with every person that they encounter.

In my own personal circumstances, after being no contact for over a year, I decided to send an email. There were things I needed to say. I did not expect or need a response. Below are some extracts from that email.

'...Your behaviour, because you were not the centre of attention, was what one would expect from a five-year-old. The emotions of a man of your nature have not matured with age. They have got stuck somewhere in your childhood and sadly that is just the way you are and will always be.

I have been told that you have moved on and found someone else. I would like to wish you all the best and hope that it works out, but I won't because I know that it will end just like all the others. You are not capable of a deep and lasting love. Your relationships will all turn into dictatorships, and if they have any self-respect they will run at the first sign of manipulation and control.'

(This relationship didn't last long.)

'When I found out what you said to my daughter at Christmas 2012 when I sent you up your Christmas dinner and I had the flu, I honestly couldn't believe that someone would be so cruel. In case you have forgotten, I will remind you. You said, 'it's not a bit of wonder your daddy did what he did.'

(My husband had taken his own life.)

'Why such a callous remark? That was truly a despicable thing to say, even for you. When I have told people that, they have all said that I am better off without someone who could say something so cruel.

You know that I saw you stalking me at the farm in June. I don't know what that was about, but I can tell you that I am very happy there and so are Ben and Asia. (My two horses.)

I came over to Tenerife in May/June to see the dentist in Los Abrigos and had to come back for a few weeks now. For the past two weeks I have been staying in the Penthouse in Duquesa del Mar, a beautiful complex. I met a lovely couple here and I have been offered an apartment here any time I want it and I intend to take them up on that offer. I know last year your son told people that I was over here stalking you when I was staying 20 miles away. When I found out I sent him a text saying that if he pushed me too far that I would see him in court. That still stands.

Remind him that it was me who booked a holiday to this area in the first place and I like it too.'

(He bought an apartment there two years ago and I was told not to go back to the area.)

'When I was speaking to (a friend) the other day, he agreed and said, 'Why shouldn't you come back here?' Exactly. God willing. I intend to.

I know you are probably ripping your hair out now by some of the things that I have said, but I really don't care. You said to me the night of my husband's funeral, 'I am not a bad man Anne.' You know, I believed that for a very long time and felt sorry for you because you had never found happiness in your life. I don't think you ever will. I know that I am not the sort of person who can be happy hating someone, but I know that for a long period of time I was very close to that……

I don't hate you now, but I don't know that I can ever forgive you. Maybe in time. I hope so. That would make me the better person if I can. The reason I have sent you this letter is for me. This is my closure.'

This worked for me. I think we all need to do what is right for each of us as an individual. That chapter of my life is now over.

BEING ALONE DOESN'T ALWAYS MEAN YOU'RE LONELY

In the course of my work on the Facebook page and website I have found that many people who have been subjected to abuse prefer to be alone for much of the time. They are fed up with a world full of people who are all out for themselves with no regard for how their behaviour or words affects those around them. People who are happy with their own company are not necessarily anti-social. They simply choose to be alone rather than subject themselves to fake people and back stabbers.

When you have been deeply hurt by someone, you often find that you distance yourself from people to protect yourself. If you don't let people get too close, they can't cause the same type of pain that you've experienced in the past. It's a form of self-preservation. Although these people may be described by some as loners, they are just quite content in their own company. Unlike a narcissist who can't abide being alone due to the lack of narcissistic supply, these people don't need others to make their lives complete. They don't need to be in the spotlight. These strong individuals can survive and thrive alone or with a small, tightknit circle of friends and/or relatives.

To become a part of their inner circle is not an easy accomplishment. They tend to be very selective when it comes to letting people get close. Due to their learning experience from their past, they often develop solid, strong boundaries. They're not going to let just anybody become a part of that circle until they've been vetted! If you are lucky enough to find yourself accepted into their inner circle, you've probably found one of the most trustworthy, solid and loyal friends that you'll ever find. These people are the rare gems of humanity that, sadly, one doesn't come across too often nowadays.

They've gained knowledge and wisdom from the rough paths that they have travelled. They have had their struggles but survived each and every stone that life threw at them and they became stronger as a result. They understand life's problems because they've been there. They'll be your rock when you need someone to lean on. Just don't betray them. They can spot a fake a mile off. That's a road well-travelled and they're not going down that route again. Once they're done, they're done and so, my friend, are you.

CHAPTER 25

RECOVERY FROM ABUSE

I am often asked, 'How long will it take to recover?' There is no straight forward answer. It's different for everyone. A lot will depend on how long you have been abused and what was done to you. Recovery from emotional abuse is going to take a lot longer than getting over a normal relationship. Some experts will say that it takes at least two years to recover from abuse, but for many, it can be much longer. I believe that to move on, you must physically get away from the narcissist in your life. It's a bit like a wound that won't heal if you keep opening it. No contact works but it is difficult. It is extremely tough to implement no contact if you have not accepted that the relationship is over, permanently.

Psychologists talk about the five stages of grief which are:

- Denial and Isolation.

- Anger.

- Bargaining.

- Depression.

- Acceptance.

It should be noted that not everyone will go through these emotions in this particular order. There is no time limit on how long each stage will take nor is it necessary to go through each one of them.

'*If only*' is an expression that we must forget. *'If only I had recognised the red flags sooner', 'If only I had of acted differently'.* Nothing you could have said or done would have changed the outcome. They are who they are. What's done is done.

'Someone who makes excuses for their bad behaviour but keeps on doing what they're doing is trying to justify what they already know they are doing wrong. There is no justification for treating others badly and they know it. They may fool some people some of the time. Don't let them fool you.'

Never be afraid to seek the help that you need. There are those who will find that therapy helps. Some people suffer from PTSD because of what was done to them.

This can be treated with the correct help and support. Others will find that going on anti-depressants for while may help. You have got to do what is right for you.

Realize that you are not the person the narcissist made you think that you are. You are much stronger than you think you are. Surround yourself with people who care. Talk to people who understand what you are going through. Don't expect people who have never been subjected to abuse to understand. They won't. You will find those who understand your pain are those who have been there.

It is essential to understand NPD and rid yourself of the belief that any of this was your fault.

You need to be able to put the pieces of the puzzle together. Understand that the narcissist is a dysfunctional human being, they were before they met you, or in the case of a parent, before you were born. Understand the immorality and wickedness that characterizes their behaviour.

You may feel that you will never be able to trust anyone ever again. You want to build walls to protect yourself and keep people out. Hard as it may be, try not to paint everyone with the same brush. There are some good people out there. There are some people who want to see you happy and not be the cause of, or rejoice in, your pain. Give those people a chance. Don't isolate yourself and cut yourself off from the world. Doing so would be letting the narcissist still have control over you once they are nothing but a distant memory. Remember that the rear-view mirror is smaller than the windscreen for a reason. Focus on what is in front of you, rather than the road you have already travelled.

POST TRAUMATIC STRESS DISORDER

PTSD is a complex disorder which is often associated with soldiers returning from combat, but it is something which is very common with people who have suffered traumatic events in their lives. It can occur at any time after the event or series of events with the person affected often having flashbacks or nightmares. Symptoms may surface at the time, months or even years later. PTSD is treatable with the correct help and support.

Symptoms of PTSD vary from person to person and may severely impact on the ability to lead a normal life. Some of the most common symptoms are listed below:

- Reliving the original trauma or event as if it is happening now.

- Flashbacks.
- Disturbed sleep, nightmares.
- Intrusive thoughts.
- Irritability.
- Inability to concentrate.
- Feelings of distress and anxiety.
- Panic attacks.
- Nervousness and feeling on edge.
- Physical symptoms – such as pain, nausea, sweating or trembling.

Some people have difficulty quelling the constant stream of negative thoughts, resulting in a continuum of questioning oneself, thus negating an ability to come to terms with the past.

It is estimated that one in three people who have suffered trauma will develop some form of PTSD.

COMPLEX PTSD

Dr Judith Herman of Harvard University suggests that a new diagnosis, Complex PTSD, is needed to describe the symptoms of long-term trauma. It may not develop for years and can cause similar symptoms to PTSD.

Cases that involve prolonged, repeated trauma may indicate a need for special treatment considerations.

What types of trauma are associated with Complex PTSD?

During long-term traumas, the victim is generally held in a state of captivity, physically or emotionally, according to Dr Herman. In these situations, the victim is under the control of the perpetrator and unable to get away from the danger.

What additional symptoms are seen in Complex PTSD?

An individual who experienced a prolonged period (months to years) of chronic victimization and total control by another may also experience the following difficulties:

- **Emotional Regulation** - May include persistent sadness, suicidal thoughts, explosive anger, or inhibited anger.

- **Consciousness** - Includes forgetting traumatic events, reliving traumatic events, or having episodes in which one feels detached from one's mental processes or body (dissociation).

- **Self-Perception** - May include helplessness, shame, guilt, stigma, and a sense of being completely different from other human beings.

- **Distorted Perceptions of the Perpetrator** - Examples include attributing total power to the perpetrator, becoming preoccupied with the relationship to the perpetrator, or preoccupied with revenge.

- **Relations with Others** - Examples include isolation, distrust, or a repeated search for a rescuer.

- **One's System of Meanings** - May include a loss of sustaining faith or a sense of hopelessness and despair.

What other difficulties are faced by those who experienced chronic trauma?

Because people who experience chronic trauma often have additional symptoms not included in the PTSD diagnosis, clinicians may misdiagnose PTSD or only diagnose a personality disorder consistent with some symptoms, such as Borderline, Dependent, or Masochistic Personality Disorder.

Care should be taken during assessment to understand whether symptoms are characteristic of PTSD or if the survivor has co-occurring PTSD and personality disorder. Clinicians should assess for PTSD specifically, keeping in mind that chronic trauma survivors may experience any of the following difficulties:

- Survivors may avoid thinking and talking about trauma-related topics because the feelings associated with the trauma are often overwhelming.

- Survivors may use alcohol or other substances to avoid and numb feelings and thoughts related to the trauma.

- Survivors may engage in self-mutilation and other forms of self-harm.

- Survivors who have been abused repeatedly are sometimes mistaken as having a 'weak character' or are unjustly blamed for the symptoms they experience as a result of victimization.

It is perfectly normal to experience intrusive thoughts after trauma, though these should improve naturally after a relatively short period of time. However, treatment should be sought if symptoms persist.

COGNITIVE BEHAVIOURAL THERAPY (CBT)

People suffering from PTSD may find this type of approach helpful in their recovery.

Cognitive Behavioural Therapy is about changing the way you think about your problems. It is not going to take the problems away, but it may change the way in which you view and deal with them. The therapy is based on talking in the hope of changing your mind-set and your behaviour.

People often become trapped with negative thinking. The aim is to break down your thoughts into little pieces which then appear to be easier to deal with and to help you understand how your thoughts may increase stress and make symptoms worse. What you once thought was overwhelming will hopefully seem to be much more manageable.

You will be able to identify the thoughts that cause you to become upset or angry and learn to suppress those thoughts and replace them with something much less distressing.

Patients who have been the target of abuse often blame themselves, holding on to feelings of guilt and shame. Cognitive Behavioural Therapy will help you understand that being abused was not your fault, that there was nothing you could have done to change things and that the responsibility lies solely with the abuser.

You may be asked to confront your traumatic memories by thinking about your experience in detail. You will learn how to cope with any distress you may feel and to no longer be afraid of those memories.

Cognitive Behavioural Therapy may produce positive results within 2 – 3 weeks.

FINDING THE RIGHT THERAPIST

Finding the right therapist is paramount. Unfortunately, not all therapists and counsellors are up to speed when it comes to the subject of narcissism and yes, you've guessed it, some therapists are narcissists. When it comes to choosing a therapist, do your homework. Going to the wrong one is like taking the wrong direction at a crossroads… You will never get to your desired destination.

Some people who attend the wrong therapist have been further traumatised by a therapist who hasn't a clue about the insidious mind games of a narcissist. Some people have been given completely wrong advice when it comes to dealing with the person who has hurt them so very deeply. Some people on the Facebook page have experienced new trauma due to being blamed and shamed by a therapist who should have studied NPD before passing any form of judgement. So please be careful. Don't be afraid to interview them to see if they are indeed the right therapist for you.

The role of a therapist is a rather powerful one in that they are in control of sessions with their clients. It is inevitable that such a position would attract some people who possess narcissistic traits themselves. If you believe that a therapist holds their position to further their own ends rather than having the best interests of their patients at heart, you may need to look elsewhere. Assess your therapist and make sure that they are the right one for you.

AUTHOR'S NOTE:

I have been studying narcissistic personality disorder for many years. It has been an interesting and yet rather disturbing learning experience. There have been people in my past who I have found it necessary to sever ties with permanently. I knew at the time that these people were not healthy to be around, but would not have been knowledgeable about the subject of NPD and simply thought of them as toxic. I know that narcissism is diagnosed by medical health professionals, but how many of us who have the misfortune to really know some of these individuals are in the best position to say that these individuals are truly narcissistic? Narcissists regularly fool therapists and mental health professionals, but they can't fool those who know them best. Today figures for NPD indicate a rise in this personality disorder but I strongly believe that these figures are somewhat underestimated. Narcissists deny and project and they do it with such credibility. They rarely admit to the fact that they are the one with a disorder. No, they are not the one with the problem. It's everyone else around them who has a problem!

I started a Facebook page, Narcissistic and Emotional Abuse, towards the end of 2014 to raise awareness about this form of abuse. In 2016, I launched the website, Narcissistic and Emotional Abuse. Both the Facebook page and website have gone from strength to strength, helping and educating people around the world about this insidious form of abuse. Both platforms give people the opportunity to talk to others who have been through similar situations. Often, people who have been abused feel isolated and alone. Speaking to other people who understand may be one of the best forms of therapy around today. Not all therapists are well educated about NPD. Sometimes the best form of support comes from people who know exactly how you feel and what you are going through.

I wrote my first article in 2014 after ending a relationship with a very controlling man. My local newspaper gave my story a double page spread and as they say, the rest is history.

I have learned a lot over the past few years. I have learned that some people who I thought were decent, honest people, were anything but. I learned not to tolerate toxic behaviour from anyone. Life is too short to put up with that sort of negativity. I've learned that it's not my job to fix those people. Their problems are their misfortune and they will have to deal with it themselves.

It has taken me a long time to get to where I am now. The devastation caused by their betrayal, and knowing that you meant absolutely nothing to these toxic individuals, will take you as low as you can possibly imagine. Getting yourself back to who you once were will take a lot of hard work and soul searching but you can get there with the help of true, genuine friends, people who will listen and not judge. For some people, that may also involve counselling.

The past ten years have been difficult at times. I lost my husband, my father, my mother, one of my horses and two of my dogs. I fell in love with someone who I thought was the man of my dreams, only to find out he was the stuff nightmares are made of. I've met people since who showed me their true colours. They are no longer a part of my life. Lastly, there was the smear campaign. All the little minions who believed the lies are long gone. The people who really know me know the truth and that's all that matters.

I have come out the other side wiser and much stronger than I ever was. You can too. Have a little faith in yourself. Time has a way of healing even the deepest of scars.

Many people lose hope. Hope is something we all need in our lives. Never give up on that. We hope for our children, we hope for a better future, we hope for our loved ones and we hope for ourselves. We all need a helping hand from time to time and sometimes we can give our time to helping others.

Don't beat yourself up for not seeing sooner this person for who they really were. Don't become your own worst enemy. It's alright not to have known then, what you know now. If you have read through this book, you will be armed with knowledge that will help you spot these toxic individuals a mile off.

Don't let the action of other people make you bitter. There are those who want to see you stumble and see you fall. Never give them that pleasure. The problems they have is with themselves. They really don't matter anymore. Don't let the pain of yesterday ruin tomorrow. Think of the past like a book, a book you didn't enjoy. Would you read it over again? I don't think so. Close it firmly and never re-read it. It's time to start a new one and a new chapter in your life and remember that you hold the pen, you decide the new beginning and the new ending.

As we get older we realise that time is short and we should spend that time with people who we love and who love us, not those who try to bring us down or get some sort of sadistic pleasure in hurting us.

Yes, I have been hurt. I've been let down by people who I trusted the most, but I've learned a lot. I used to take people as I found them and generally thought they were decent people unless they proved otherwise. Now, I am a little more careful. I'll reserve my judgements for a time. I suppose that's self-protection, but it works. Not everyone is who they first appear to be. That's ok. I'll keep those people at a distance. I have made new friends and resurrected some old ones. My two children and my friends are more than enough. My life is full. The Facebook page and website have helped many, many people. I am grateful for all the lovely messages and emails that I receive. They make the effort and hard work over these past few years so very worthwhile.

Do I regret the love that I gave to the wrong people? No. There is no doubt that they have helped me become the person I am today, stronger and a hell of a lot wiser.

To all those going through hard times at the moment. We can all get over this. Have a little faith in yourself. It is not a sign of weakness to seek help. It is a sign of strength to admit to a problem, address it and seek whatever help you need. It is never too late.

Some people ask me if there is light at the end of the tunnel. Hell, yes. You just have to remember to switch on the light!

The narcissist has turned your world upside down and started a fire that burned your heart. Don't let it be a fire you never put out.

Love to all, Anne

QUOTES BY ANNE McCREA FROM THE FACEBOOK PAGE AND WEBSITE

When someone is being bullied, don't say, 'It's none of my business.' It is. It's everyone's business.

You don't owe your loyalty to people who deliberately hurt you or those who don't care if they do.

A favourite tactic of a narcissist is to disappear from a relationship or friendship without any notice or warning. This method of terminating a relationship is their ultimate form of power and control. They have decided to cease all communication, not unlike a small child putting their fingers to their ears in an act of defiance, refusing to listen and refusing to talk. The level of emotional maturity is around the same.

A narcissist lives by a certain set of rules otherwise known as 'Double Standards'. You will be expected to abide by these rules. However, these exact same rules won't apply to them.

Sometimes, as hard as it may be, we have to accept that some people are evil to the core and always will be. Don't waste your time looking for the good that simply isn't there.

Anyone who sides with an abuser, criticizes, abandons or ostracizes a target is every bit as guilty as the abuser. So too are those who participate in a smear campaign. Some people are weak and tend to go with the crowd instead of standing up for what is right. Abusers often side with abusers. It takes strength to stand alone.

Narcissistic rage is always simmering just beneath the surface... An unprovoked display of anger and rage, similar to a temper tantrum of a three-year-old child. When the narcissist tells the story, there's going to be a villain and it's not going to be them.

One of the hardest things in life is learning that those who you trusted the most, those who could never question your loyalty, showed you that trust and loyalty are not always guaranteed. Never think that losing those sort of people is a loss. You don't need what they're offering. It ain't worth having.

When the narcissist and their family try to destroy your reputation to protect the narcissist and conceal their despicable behaviour, they are enabling abuse. They become accomplices permitting and prolonging abuse either by their actions or failure to take a stand.

There's a big difference between people who stop talking to you because of their desire to punish and control and those who stop talking because they are hurt and need to look after themselves.

If they can love you today and behave like you don't exist tomorrow, there's something seriously flawed with their character.

It is ok to walk away from toxic people, people who hurt you and don't show you respect.
It's not selfish. It's self-respect. You don't owe anyone an explanation or taking care of yourself.

There is nothing more dangerous to a narcissist than the voice of an honest person who is not afraid to speak.

Toxic people will try to destroy the reputation of those who they know can crush them with the truth.

Someone who really cares for you will never get any sort of pleasure from seeing you hurt and knowing they are the cause of your pain. Love doesn't work that way.

I've got to a stage in my life where I know what's good and what's bad. If you can't add value to my life, then you ain't gonna be a part of it.

A toxic person's mood will blow hot and cold. They can change from being evil and hateful, to charming and pleasant, in the blink of an eye. The audience is often a deciding factor in their choice of behaviour. Don't be fooled into thinking they've changed for the better when you see a dramatic change. Those old ways are coming back! Maybe not today, maybe not next week, but believe me when I say, they are simply 'on hold'.

When I start to think I'm missing you, I realize I'm just missing the person I wanted you to be.

Never shoulder the blame for someone else's bad behaviour. Let them take responsibility
For the shit they do. That's not your burden to carry.

You know you are strong when you don't need validation from anyone or anyone's approval for being yourself.

Ungrateful and toxic people complain about the things you haven't done instead of being grateful for all the things you did. Don't waste your precious time trying to do everything for someone who appreciates nothing or for someone who suffers from selective amnesia.

A narcissist will use your reaction to their abuse to prove how unstable you are. They will push you to your limits and tell other people only part of the story, conveniently leaving out what they did. Your reaction was a normal reaction to an abnormal amount of bullshit.

Make today be the last day that you care about people who have shown you that they don't.

There are those who will ignore you when you need them most and then there are those who will be there for you. No matter what and you don't even have to ask. Know who to hold on to and who to let go.

There'll come a time when you see them for who they really are. You'll stop excusing their behaviour and you'll know that they don't deserve another chance and when that time comes, you'll know that you deserve so much more than they can ever give.

A narcissist is a master of manipulation. They avoid accountability for their bad behaviour by blaming others for causing it.

One of a narcissist's greatest fears is exposure of their lies and destructive behaviour. The more they can discredit you, the less likely you are to be believed. True friends will stand by you. Forget about the others. They're not worth a second thought.

People talk of a narcissist's uncontrollable rage. Much of the time they are in complete control of their rage, confining their tantrums to behind closed doors. Maintaining their image is paramount. No witnesses, no evidence.

Be patient. No one can hide from the truth. It's like oil on water. It will come to the surface eventually. Just sit back and give it time.

You know they are going to talk about you and it's not going to be good. People will judge you, not because they know you, but because of what they have heard. Some who know you will listen to the lies and the gossip and do you know something? None of it matters. You know the truth. People believe what they want to believe. Let them.

Don't let a dysfunctional person make you believe that their behaviour is normal. There's nothing normal about someone who, without reason, replaces conversation with silence, truth with lies, approval with contempt and respect with scorn. That just ain't normal!

You can be a kind and empathetic person without letting people walk all over you. Set your boundaries and don't let anyone cross them. It's not being selfish. It's just taking care of yourself. There will be those who overstep the mark and won't respect the standards you have set. Let them go if they can't raise their standards to meet yours.

Not everyone who you think is your friend is a true friend. Be careful who you share your secrets with. There will be some who will happily use that information against you. Some will say that they have your back, but they will be the first to stab you in it. Take your time and let them prove they are worthy of your trust. Time has a way of exposing fake people. Know your circle. Keep it tight.

Don't worry about exposing fake people and liars. Give them some time and they'll expose themselves.

Your future doesn't lie with the pain you leave behind. Walking away from all the bullshit
And the people who create it does not make you a bad person.

Your strength doesn't come from the easy times. It comes from all the tough battles you faced, the ones you fought and won.

The narcissist's fan club will change over and over as people come and go. The lifespan of a flying monkey in the narcissist's world is often limited. It's a mug's game. They are expendable and will be replaced when they can no longer be controlled or manipulated or when they are of no further use.

Don't be afraid of being judged for speaking the truth. People are going to judge you whether you stay silent or speak out. The weak and insecure will judge. The wise will listen.

Life is better when you distance yourself from negative people.

There'll come a time when you see them for who they really are... A phoney, a liar and a loser. And when that time comes, their opinions and even the mention of their name won't mean a thing.

I don't hold grudges, but I hold on to my memories. Those memories prepare me for if or when we should ever meet again.

And the Oscar for best actor goes to the narcissist for their brilliant portrayal of a victim.

Some people will trade in their honesty and moral principles just to be the centre of attention.
Avoid these people.

The narcissist likes to play FORGIVE AND FORGET, where you forgive and forget and they keep on doing what they're doing. Know when to stop playing.

Whichever direction you choose, there may be people from your past who try to come back into your life. Be very careful. They've already shown you exactly who they are. Let them stay in your past.

Don't fall for their attempts to resurrect the past. It's futile. Protect yourself, protect your heart. The outcome has already been decided. You set the standards of how you will let people treat you. Don't let people jump in and out of your life and treat you with disrespect.
Set your standards high and keep them there.

Don't let faded memories of a time long gone take you down that wrong road again.
You know where it leads and you know where it ends. It's gonna take you right back to where you've been.

Never let anyone who is critical and controlling make you feel bad about yourself. When someone deliberately tries to hurt you, there is clearly something wrong with them, not you. Normal, mentally healthy human beings don't intentionally hurt others to feel good about themselves.

There are some people who will never learn from their mistakes. They never see a problem with their behaviour and how they treat people. When people leave them, and they eventually do, they'll always find someone else to blame.

Narcissists are more concerned about impressing people outside the home than impressing those who live within.'

When we think of loss, we think of losing something precious or someone who adds value to our lives. Now, think of what you've 'lost', someone who controls, someone who lies, someone who denigrates, someone who humiliates, an abuser without remorse. That's not a loss. That's a gain.

Let me get this straight... You're gonna keep on lying after being caught out in the lies, denying the lies with more lies and then wonder why people aren't gonna believe you.

Some people are evil to their very core. They take pleasure in the hurt and pain that they inflict and then blame their victim for causing it.

Sometimes it's better not to argue. Let them delude themselves. Walk away and let them be wrong.

You have the power to give yourself closure. You don't need anyone's approval. Walk away with your head held high. That's your closure and it's all that you need.

The narcissist's 'goodbye'.
I'll slip away and pretend you don't exist. You'll never know why I left. I don't owe you an explanation. You'll text and call but I won't answer. If I see you, I'll look the other way.
Don't try to get closure from me. You won't get it. You're no longer a part of my world... for now. That's how I say goodbye each and every time. Don't close the door though.
I may come back some day, just to do it all over again.

Forget about revenge. Redirect your energy and focus on yourself. You've got what it takes
To move on and be happy. They don't.

I've got to a point in my life where I don't try to impress anyone. I can't stand hypocrites, bullies and people who lie, those who don't care how their words or actions hurt other people and those who are cruel to animals. Take me as I am. If you like me, that's fine,
And if you don't, well... I'm not really that bothered. Narcissists don't have a desire to stop doing what they're doing. What they do have are excuses and blaming everyone else for their bad behaviour.

On the inside of some people you think you know, hides a person you don't.

If you've got to pretend I'm a shitty person so that you don't feel bad about the shady stuff you did, go ahead. I'm not bothered. Bless your delusional little heart.

Don't ever consider yourself to be broken, maybe a little stuck now and then, but never broken.

Love and protect your pack. Know your enemies. Bow to no earthly master. Fear no man.

Give respect to those who earned it. Respect yourself and take no shit.

It's better to be in the company of people who make mistakes and admit to them than those 'perfect' folk who make none.

I've learned a lot these last few years. I've learned that things don't always turn out the way I planned or the way I thought they should be. I've learned that things go wrong in life that don't always get fixed. There are some things that are broken and are meant to stay that way. I've learned that I can get through the tough times with truth and honesty on my side.

I've learned that some people who I thought were my friends were just passing through. They have shown me who I do not want to be. They will, forever, be a part of my past but never be a part of my future. And that's ok. STOP looking back, taking back and going back.
Your future's in front of you, not behind you.

The content in this book is for your information. It is not intended to be a substitute for professional advice from your health professional or counsellor.

REFERENCES

Page 8 – Mayo Clinic Staff, Mayo Clinic: Narcissistic Personality Disorder, [Online], (Nov 2014). Accessed February 2016.

Page 36 - Dr George K Simon, https://www.powerofpositivity.com/7-signs-someone-trying-psychologically-manipulate/, [Online], 2009-2015 Power of Positivity.
Accessed August 2017

Page 74 - New Oxford English Dictionary, [Online], 2017 Oxford University Press
Accessed August 2017

Page 90 - Cambridge English Dictionary, [Online], Cambridge University Press 2017.
Accessed August 2017

Page 93 - Patrick Carnes, The Betrayal Bond. Health Communications. (1998).

Page 115 - Herman, J. Trauma and recovery: The aftermath of violence from domestic abuse to political terror. Basic Books (1997).

Page 113 - US Department of Veterans Affairs, PTSD: National Center for PTSD, [Online], 17 August 2015. Accessed February 2016.

Printed in Great Britain
by Amazon